The Simple Pleasure of Bike Ride;

Today, people living in the financial city of Mumbai in India, struggling with amplified office life and working hours; like to unleash themselves and participate in activities they find pleasure in.

There are people from different businesses and backgrounds who find the common pleasure in motorbike riding and they either ride solo or have incorporated their own riding groups.

At times, they take up short rides lasting for a few hours, to riding as long as for 20-25 days across the country or even internationally. The riders, sometimes explore small villages and scenic landscapes en-route.

I've covered this series along with my friend, Shubham Walavalkar, at his native, Malvan, a coastal town in the State of Maharashtra, in India. He is 20 years old and is a mass media student, studying at a college in Mumbai, India. This was entirely an unplanned trip to his native, where he usually goes to unleash himself with a bike ride to serene locations, with the simple motive of pleasure.

- Sudeep Mehta

THE SIMPLE PLEASURE of BIKE RIDE

A Photo Series by
SUDEEP MEHTA

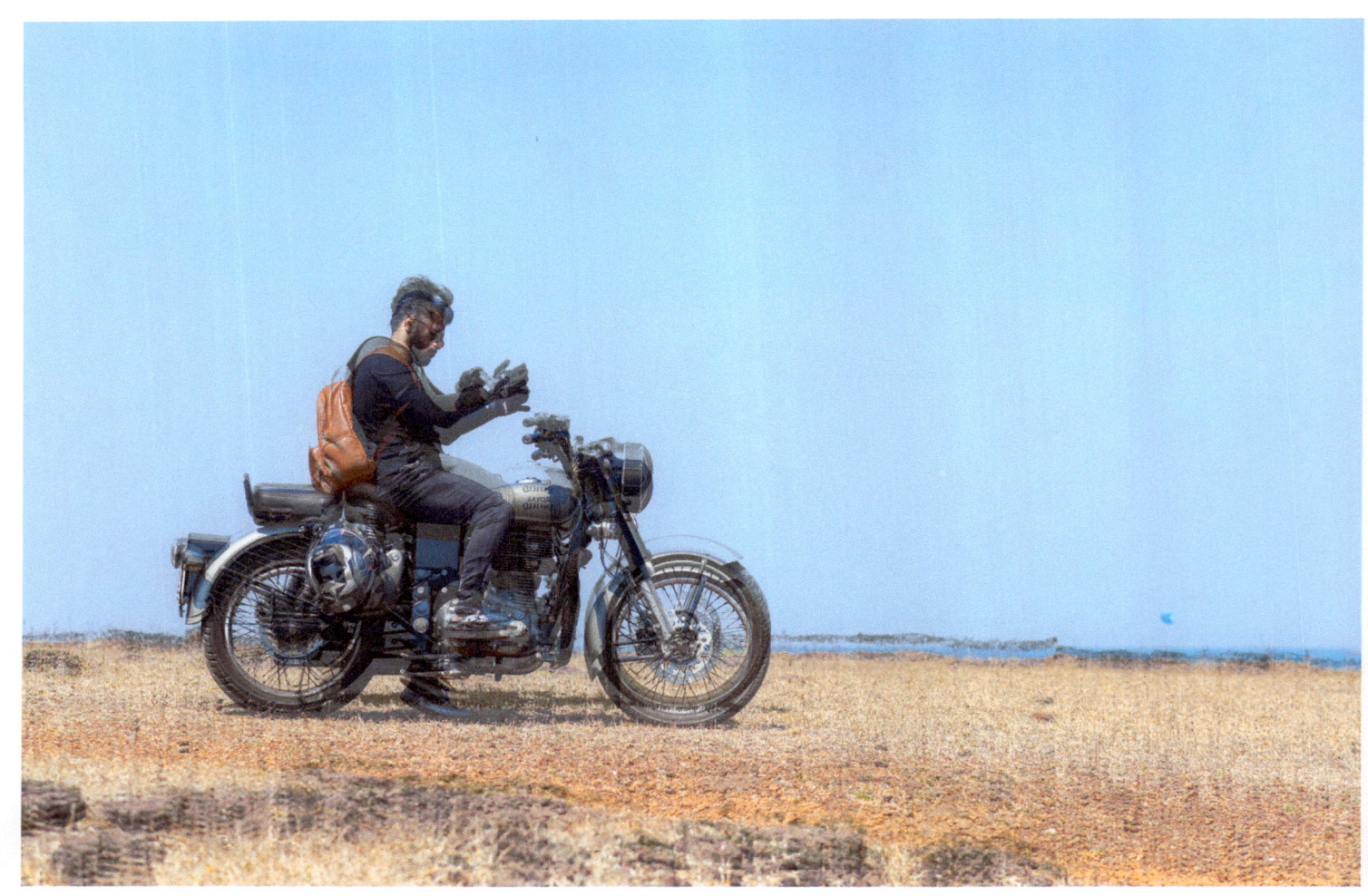

Gearing Up
Malvan, India. February 2020

Sarjekot
Malvan, India. February 2020

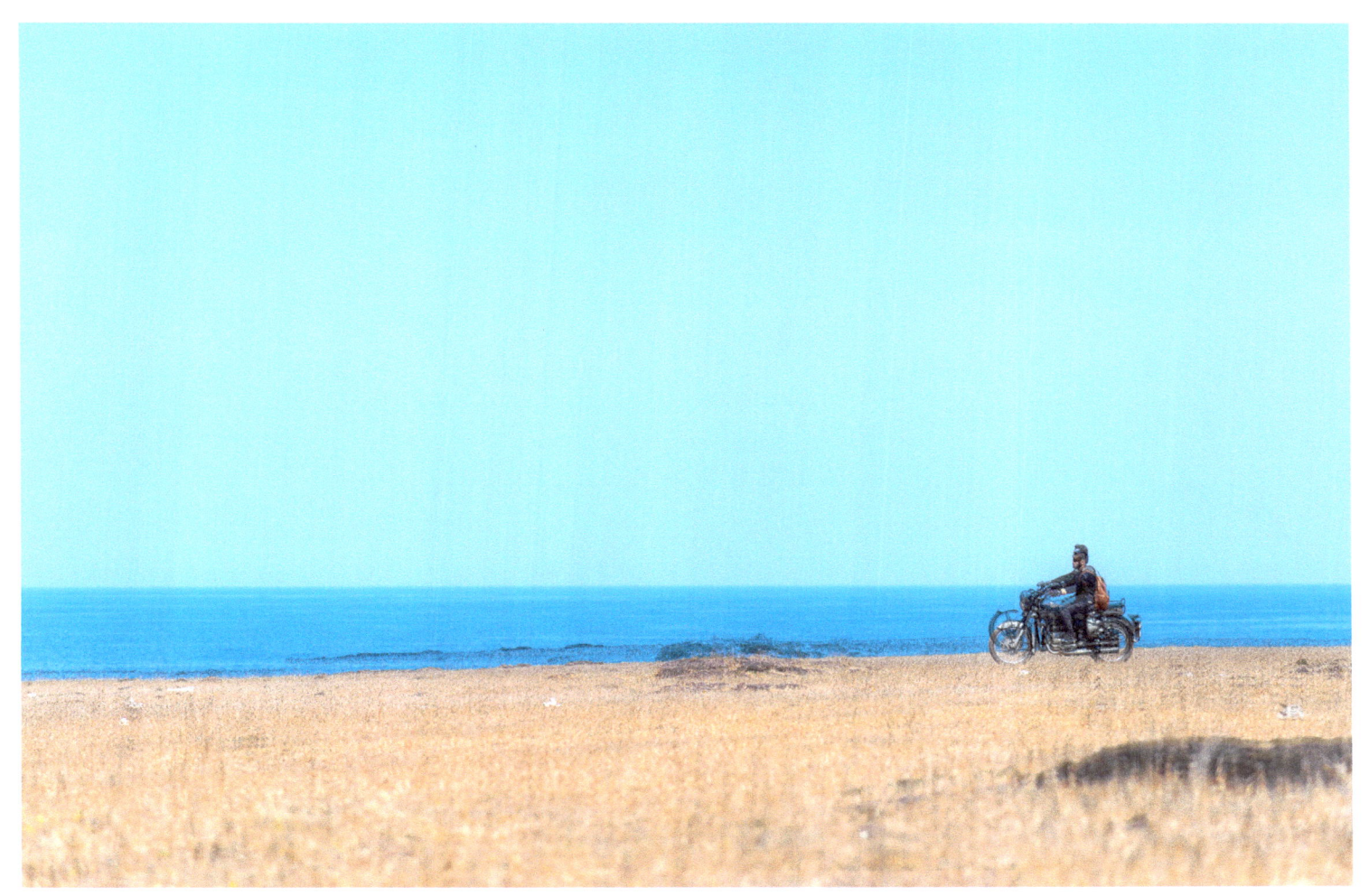

The Cliff, Sarjekot
Malvan, India. February 2020

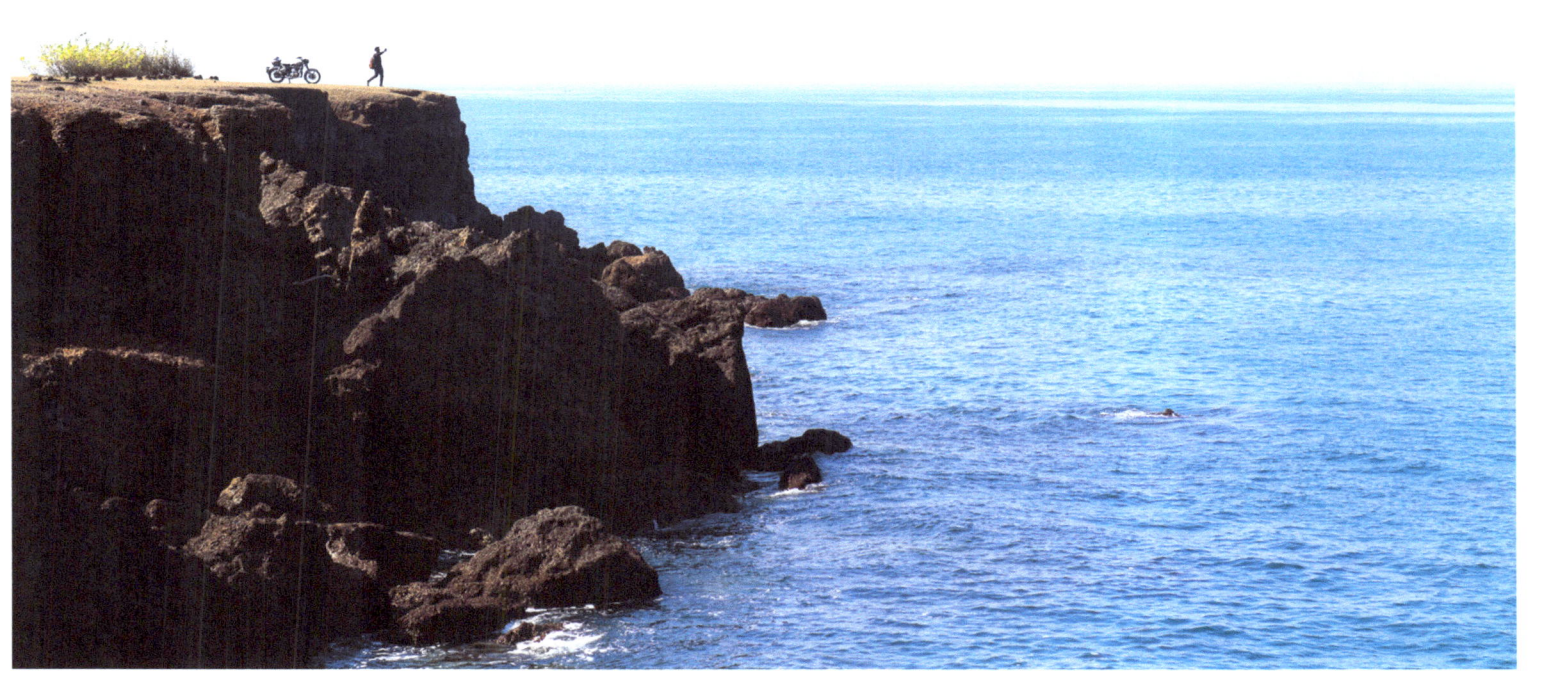

The Cliff, Sarjekot (Ariel View)
Malvan, India: February 2020

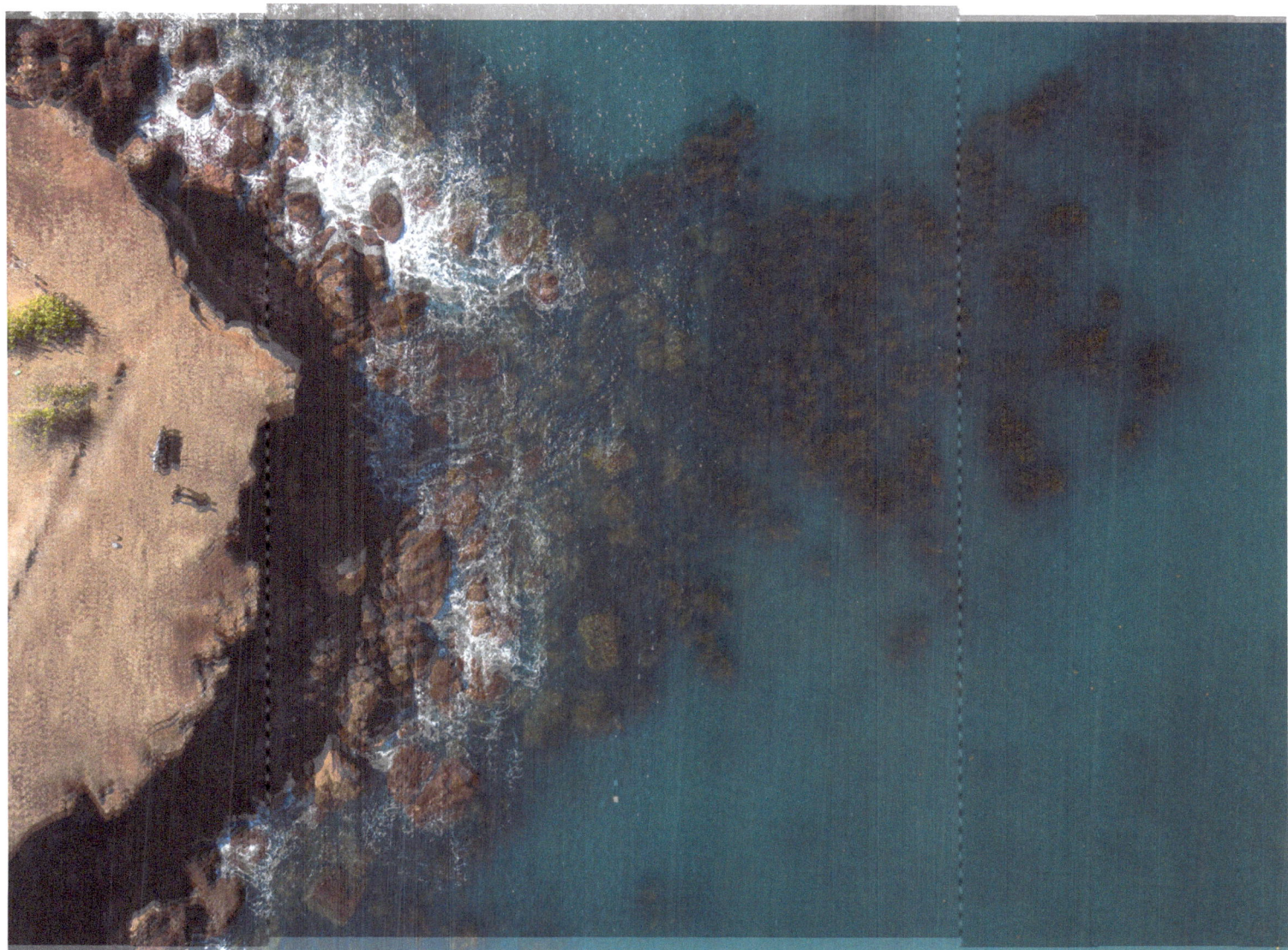

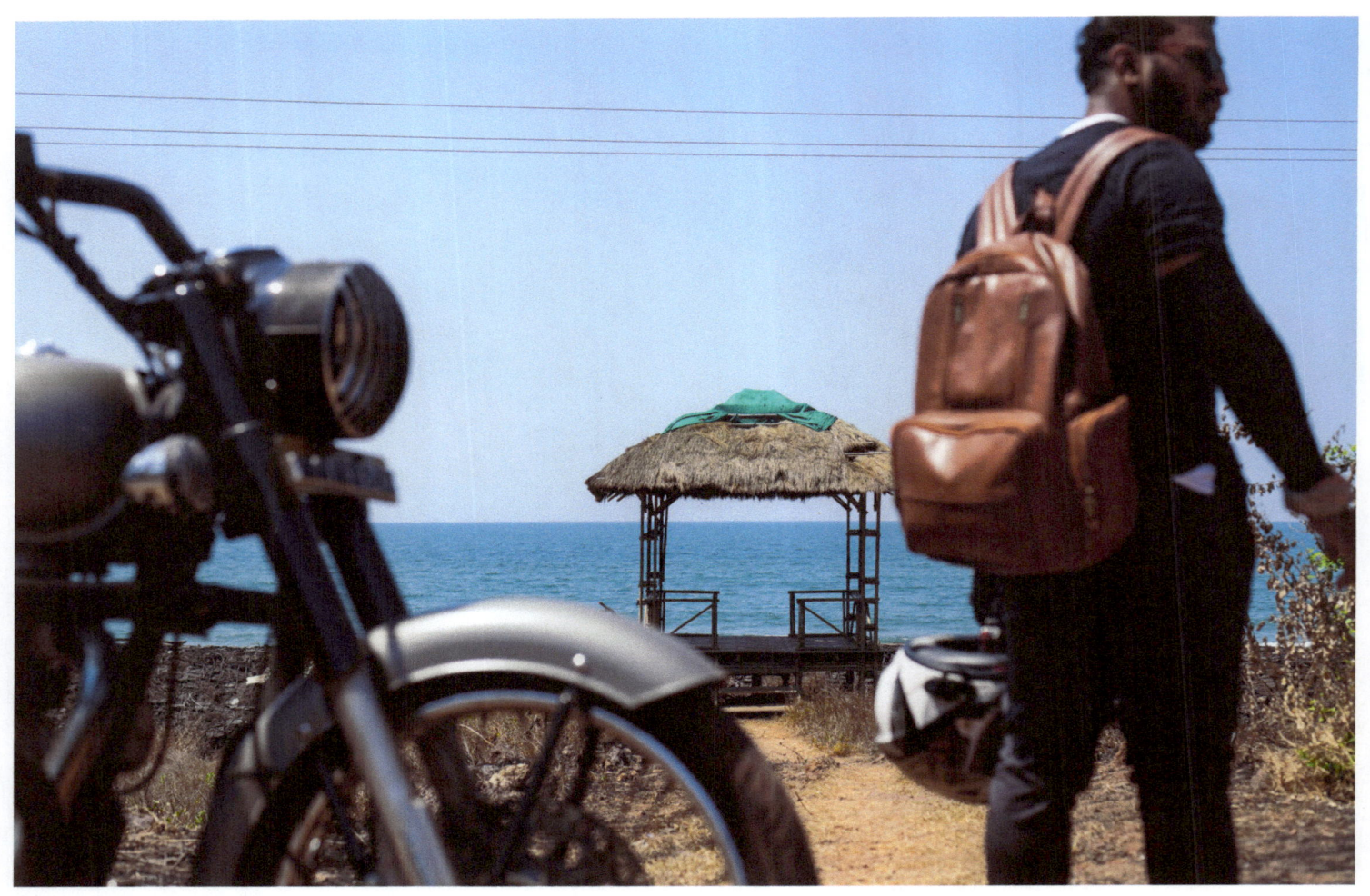

Finding A New Spot, Talashil
Malvan, India. February 2020

Gazeo By The Beach, Talashil
Malvan, India. February 2020

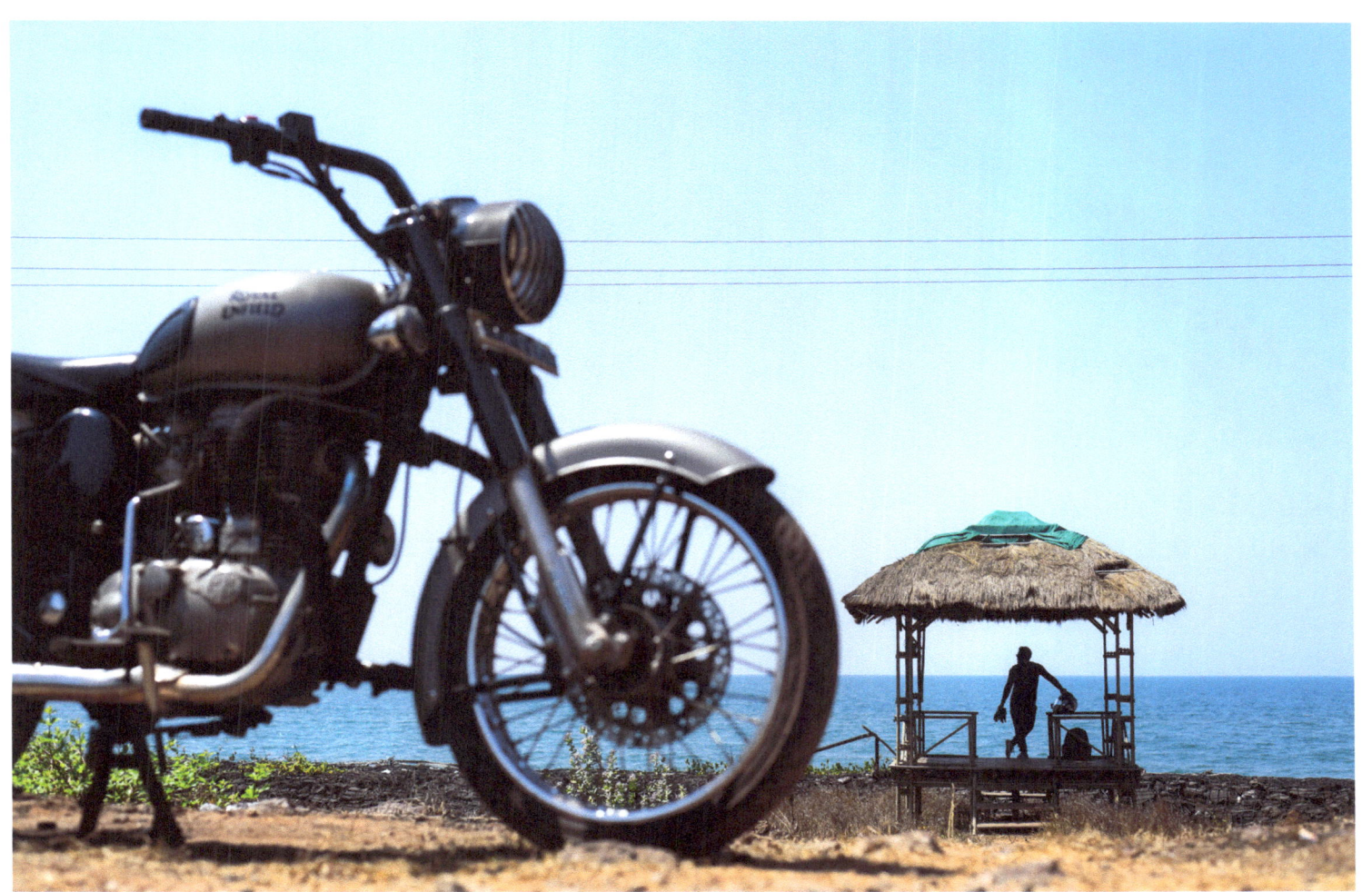

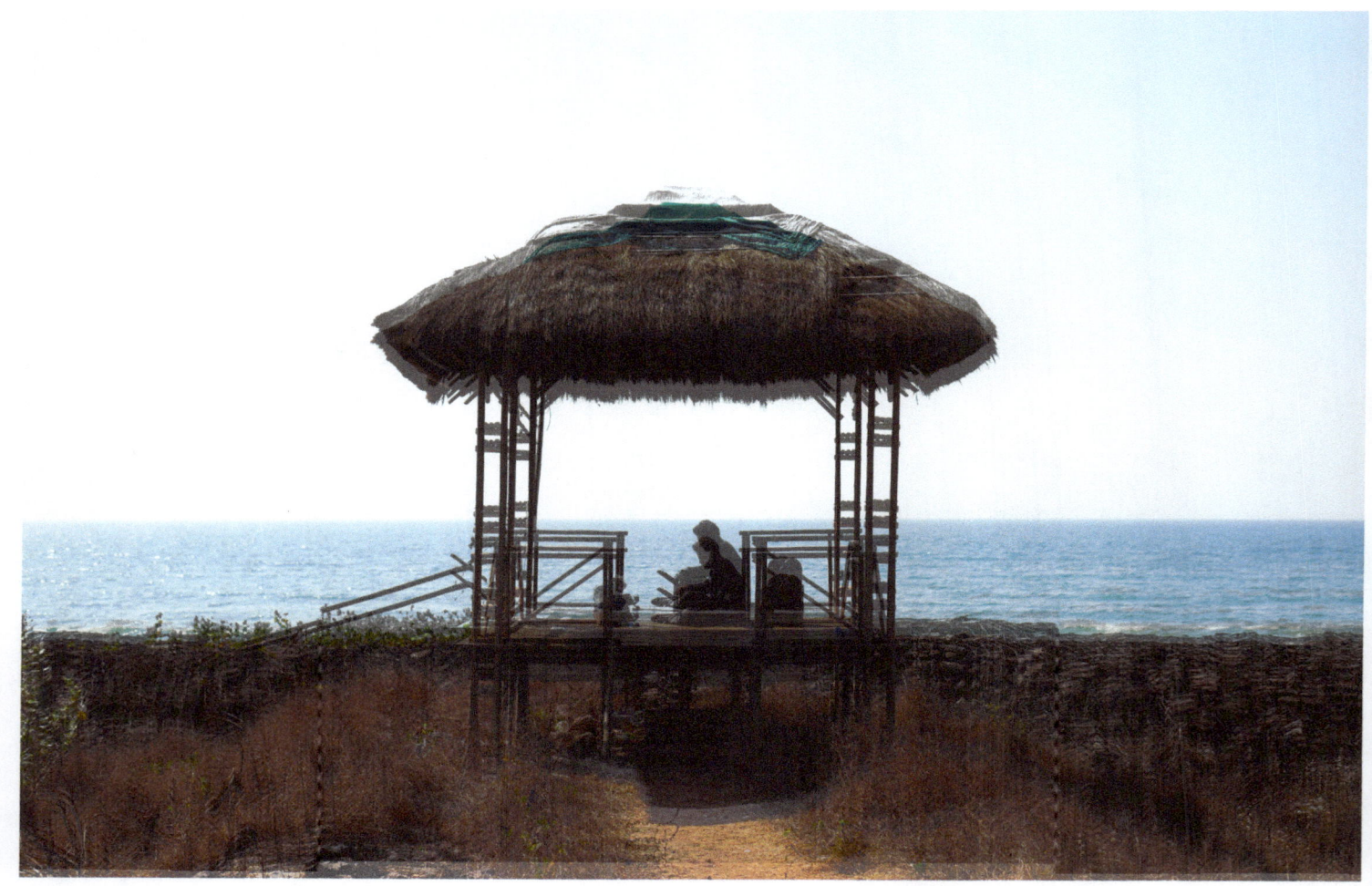

Gazebo By The Beach, Talashil Malvan, India. February 2020

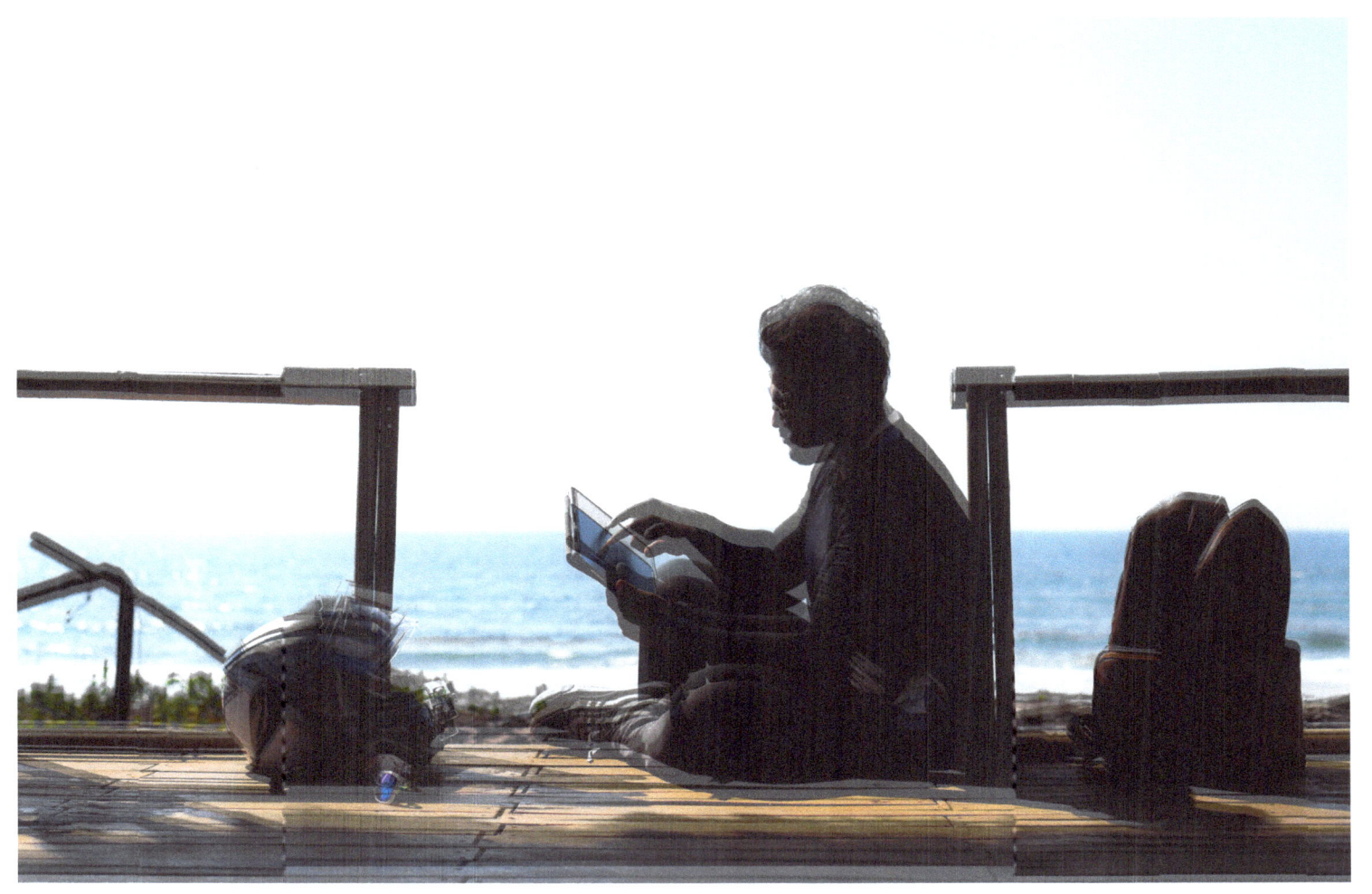

Gazed By The Beach, Talashil
Malvan, India. February 2020

Kalawal Bridge, Hadi (Ariel View)
Malvan, India. February 2020

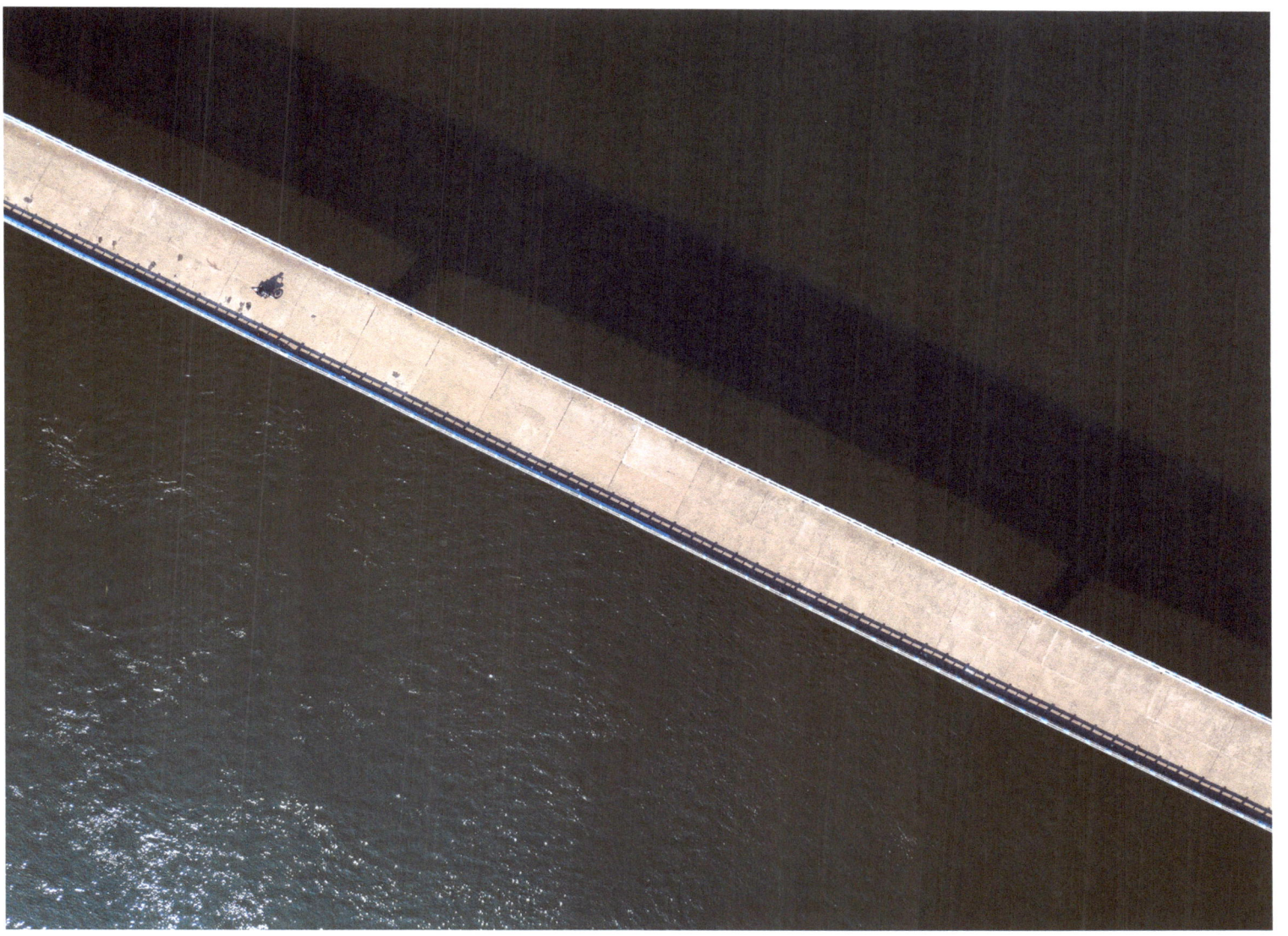

Speed & Motion; Hadi Malvan, India: February 2020

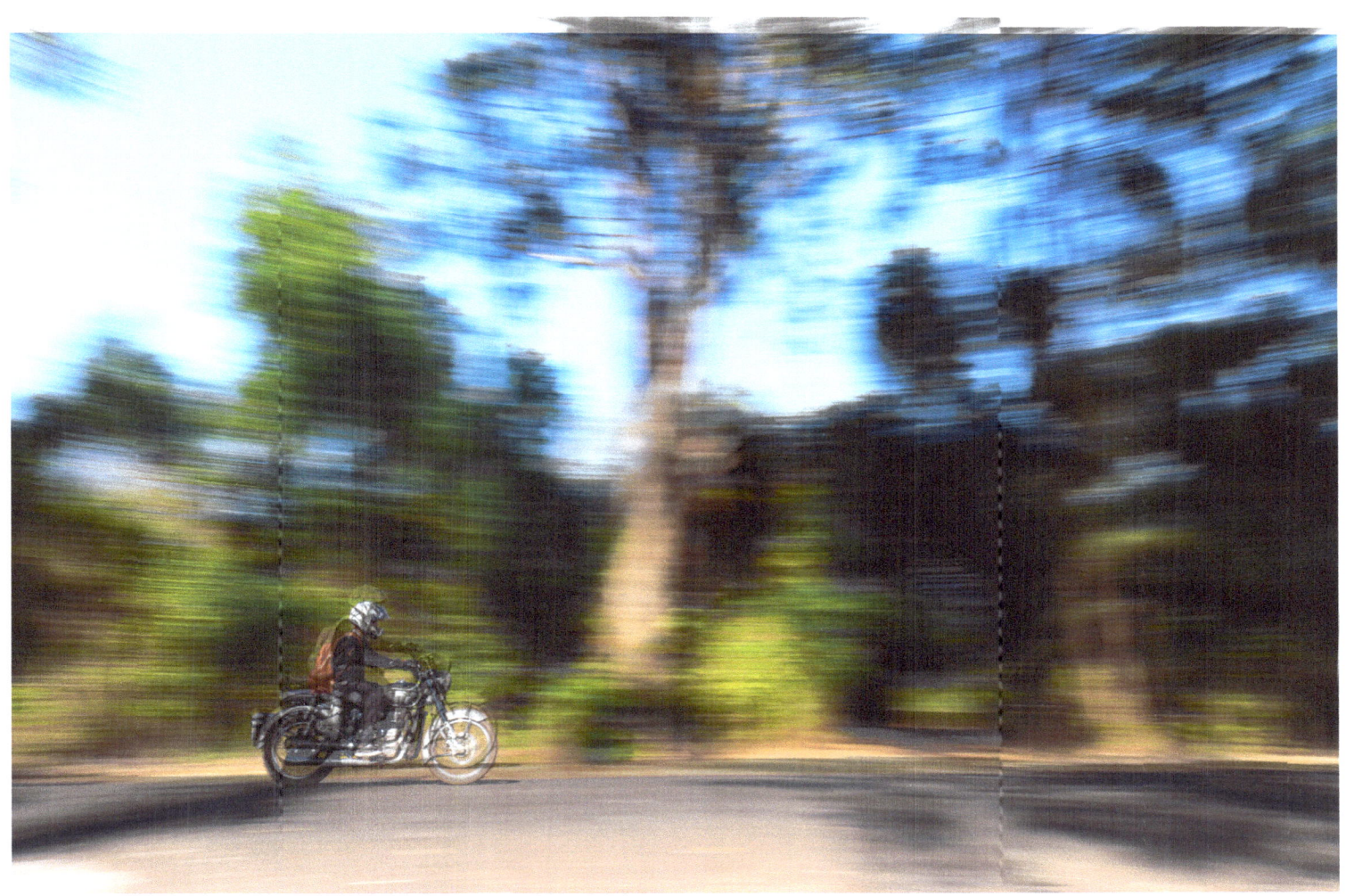

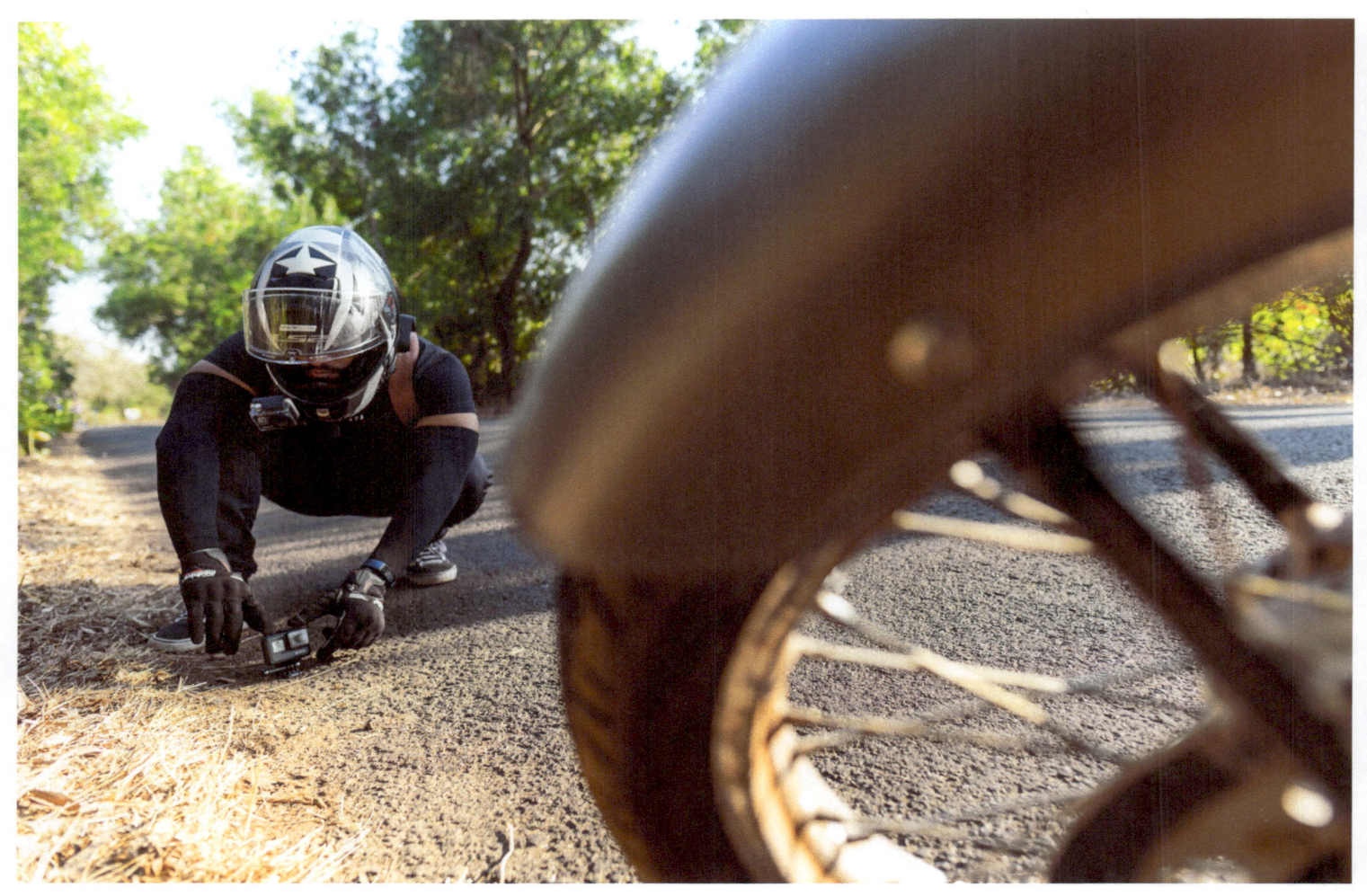

The Remote Selfie, Hadi
Malvan, India. February 2020

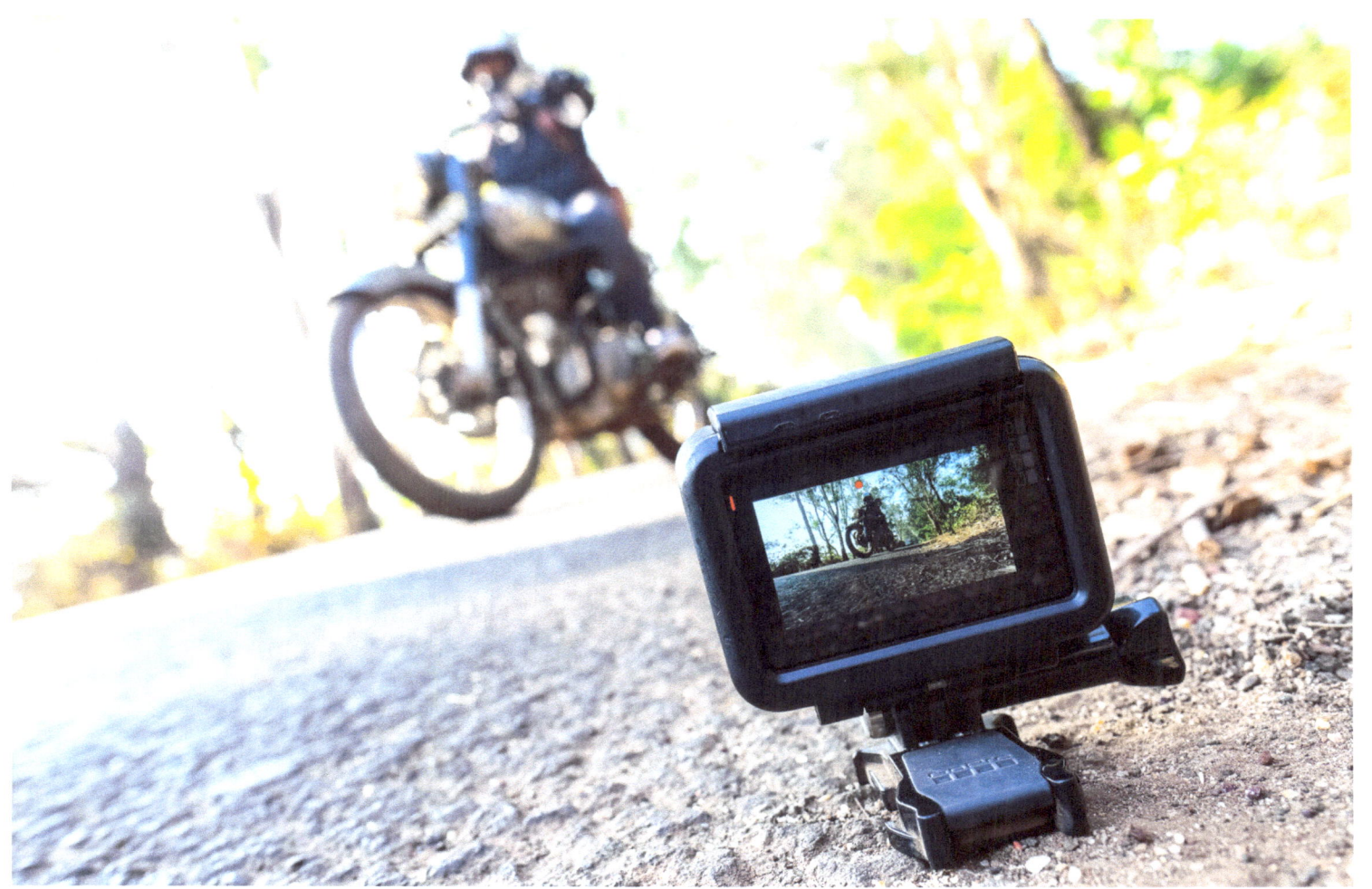

The Remote Selfie, Hadi
Malvan, India. February 2020

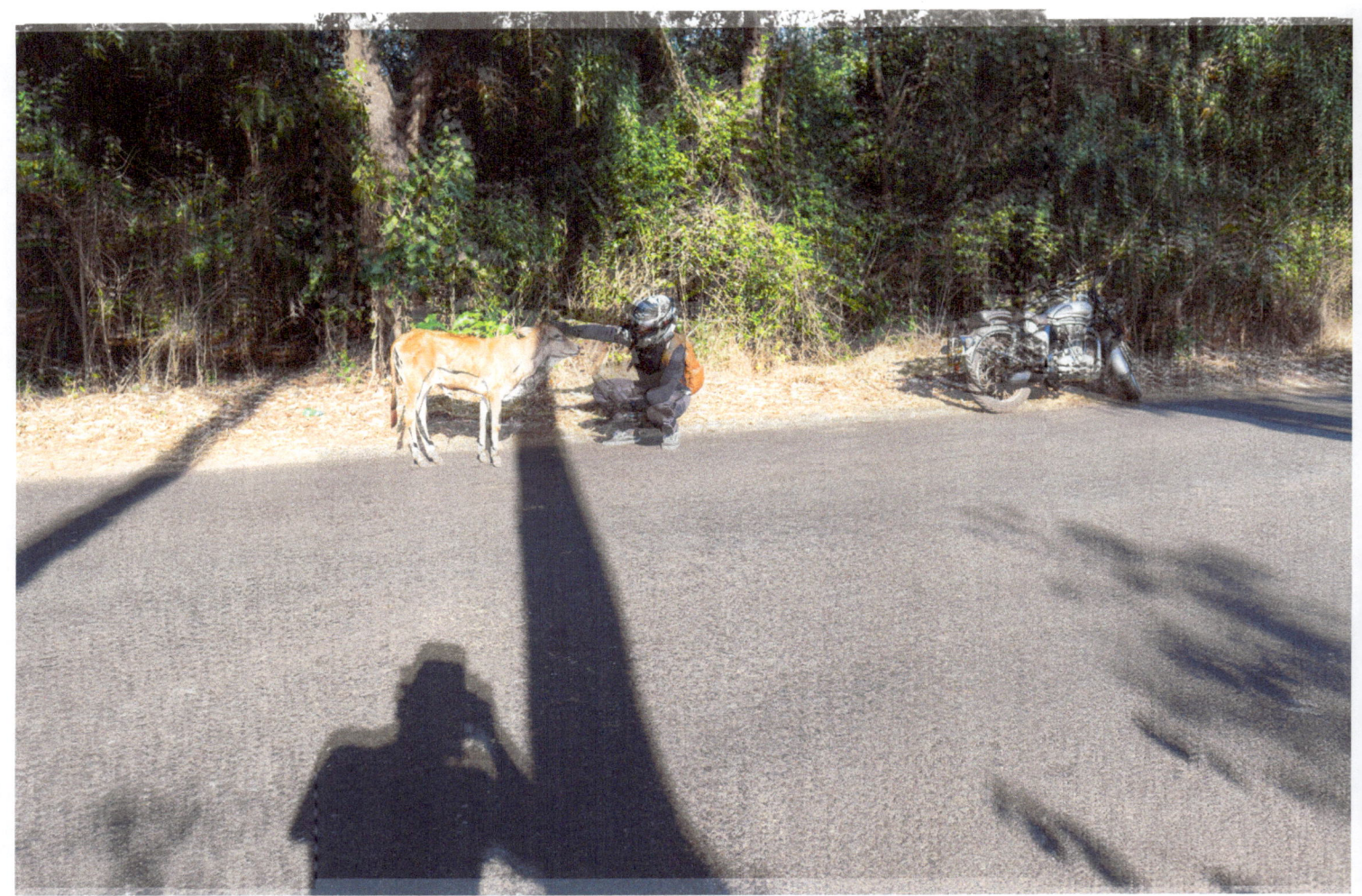

Cattle On The Roads, Hadi
Malvan, India. February 2020

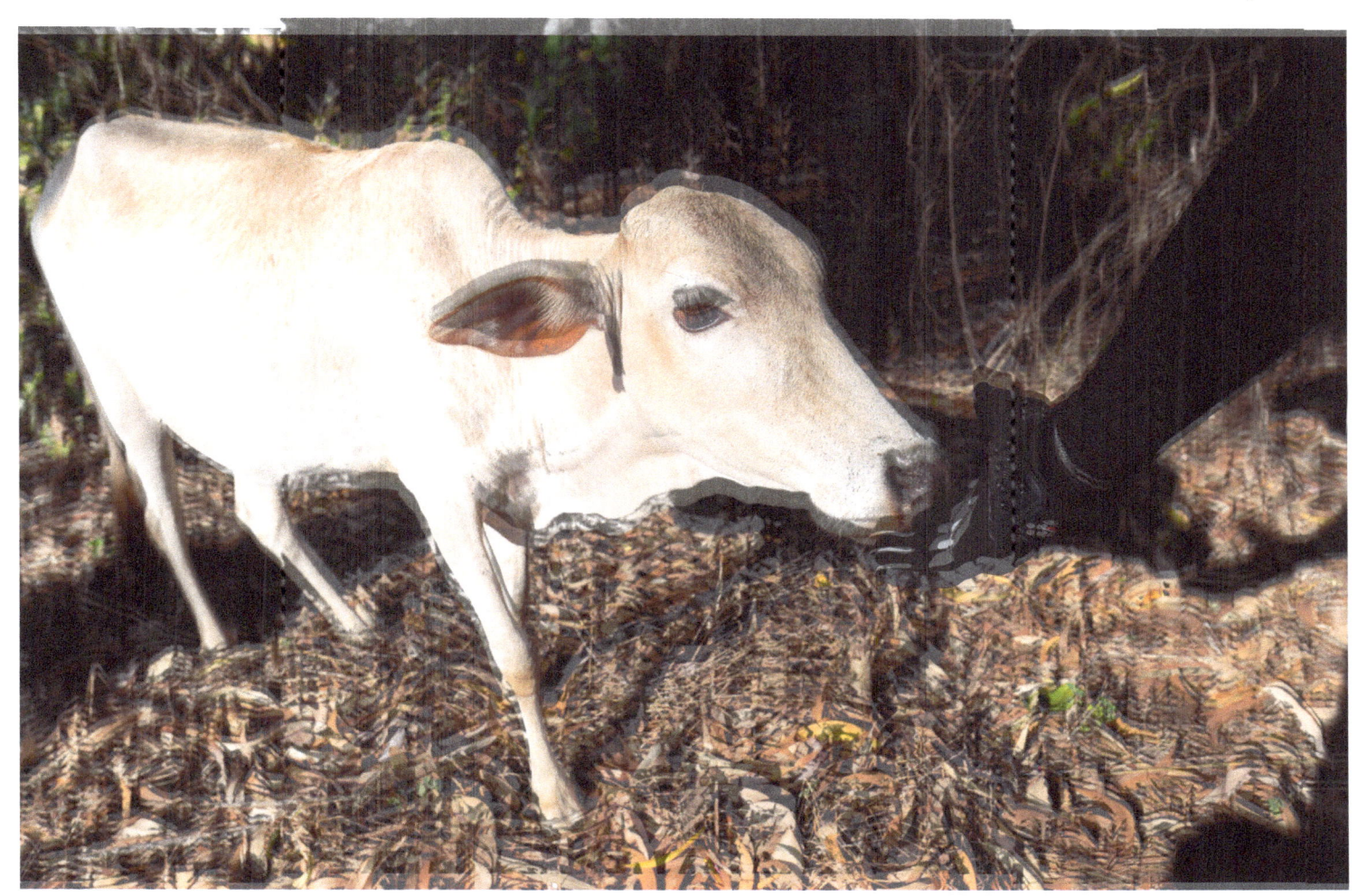

Cattle On The Roads, Hadi Malvan, India. February 2020

The Leopard Dog, Hadi
Malvan, India. February 2020

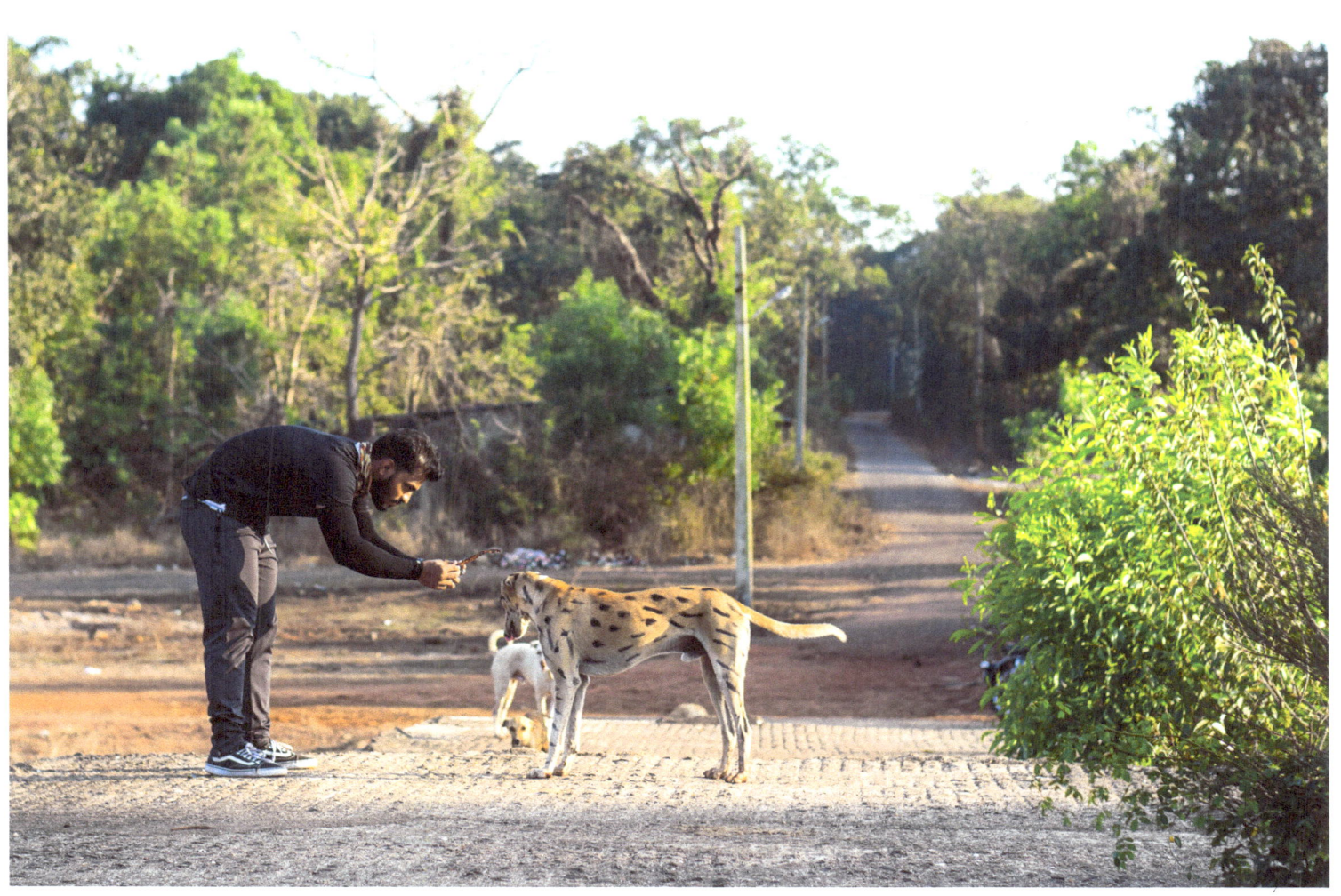

The Leisure Time, Hadi Malvan, India: February 2020

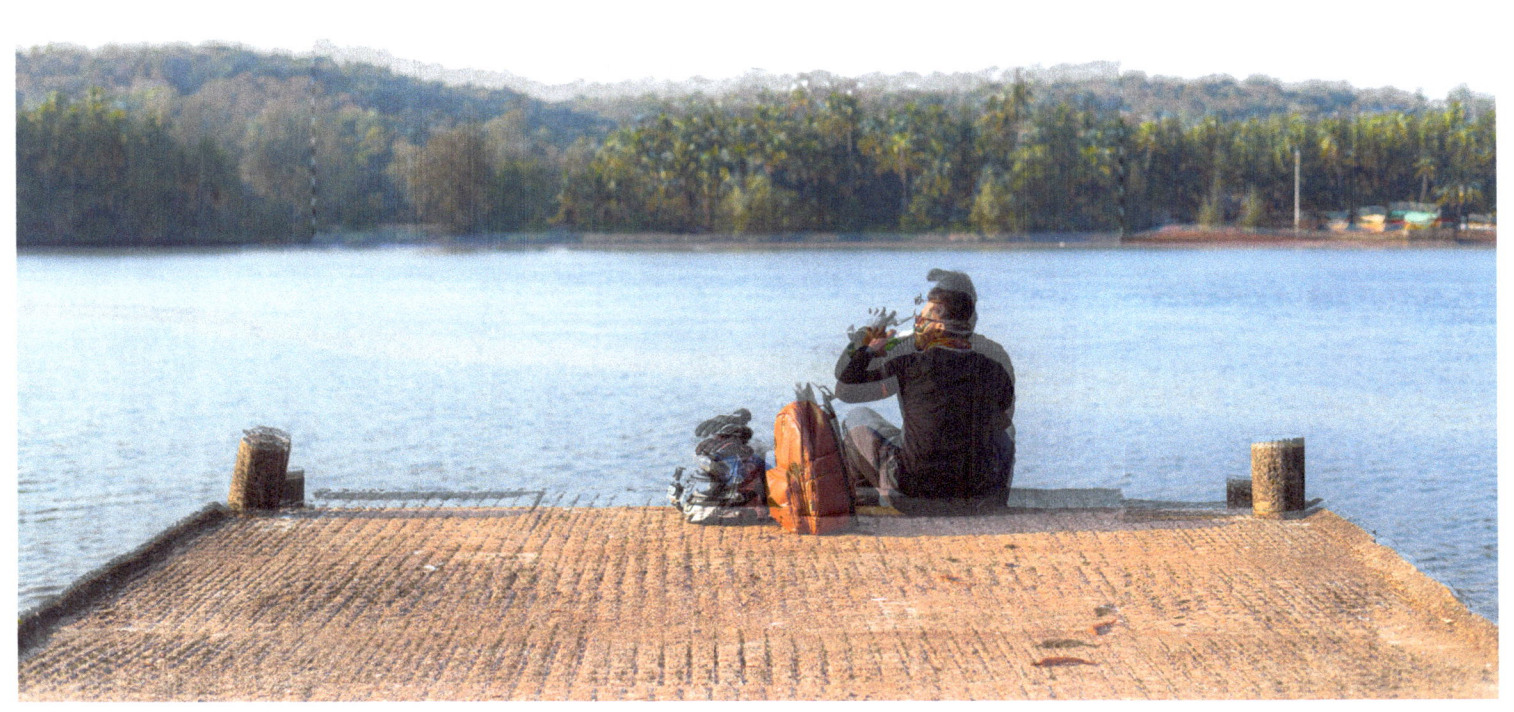

Sunset, Hadi
Malvan, India. February 2020

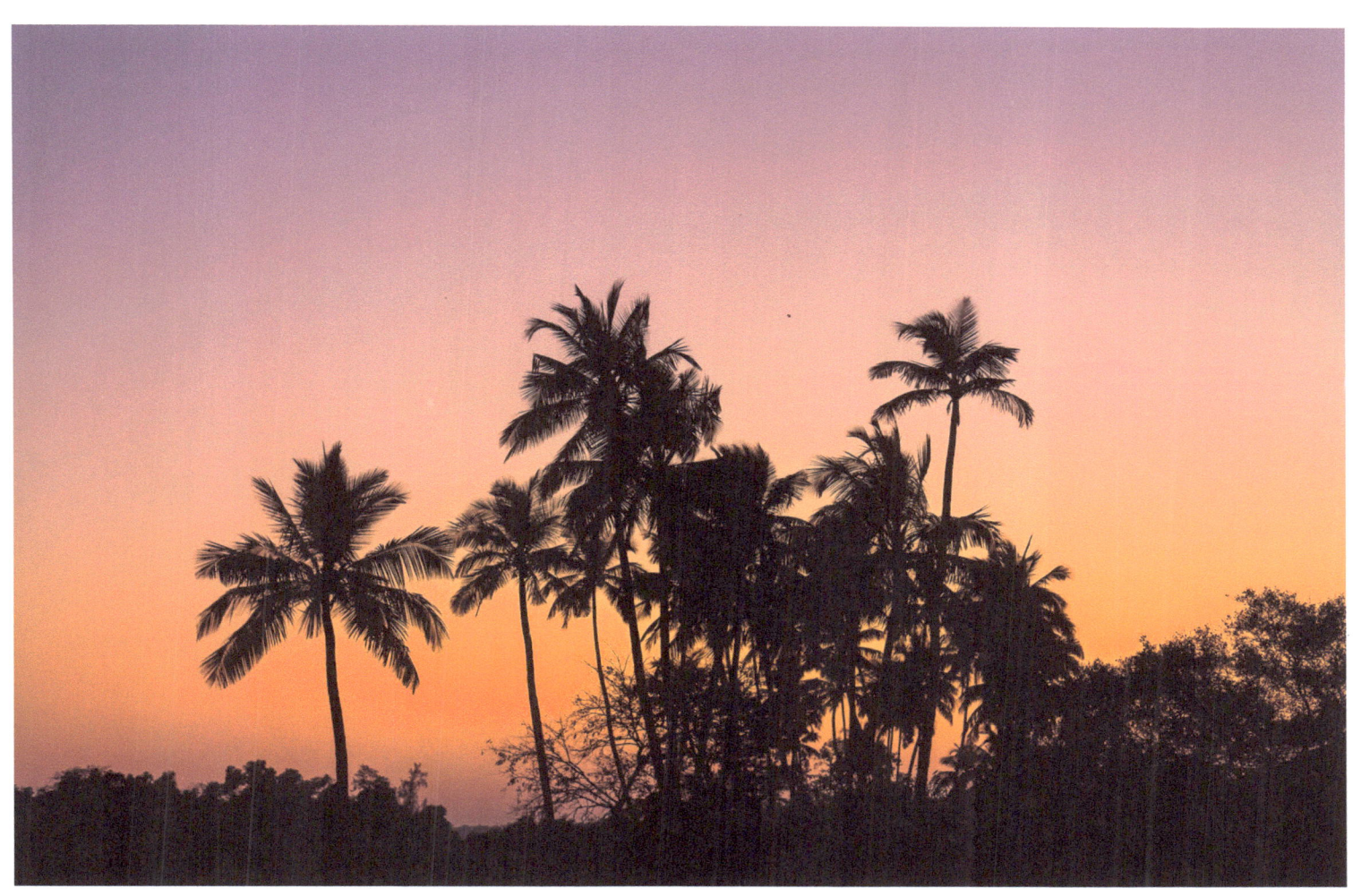

Shubham's Farm-House, Kolamb
Malvan, India: February 2020

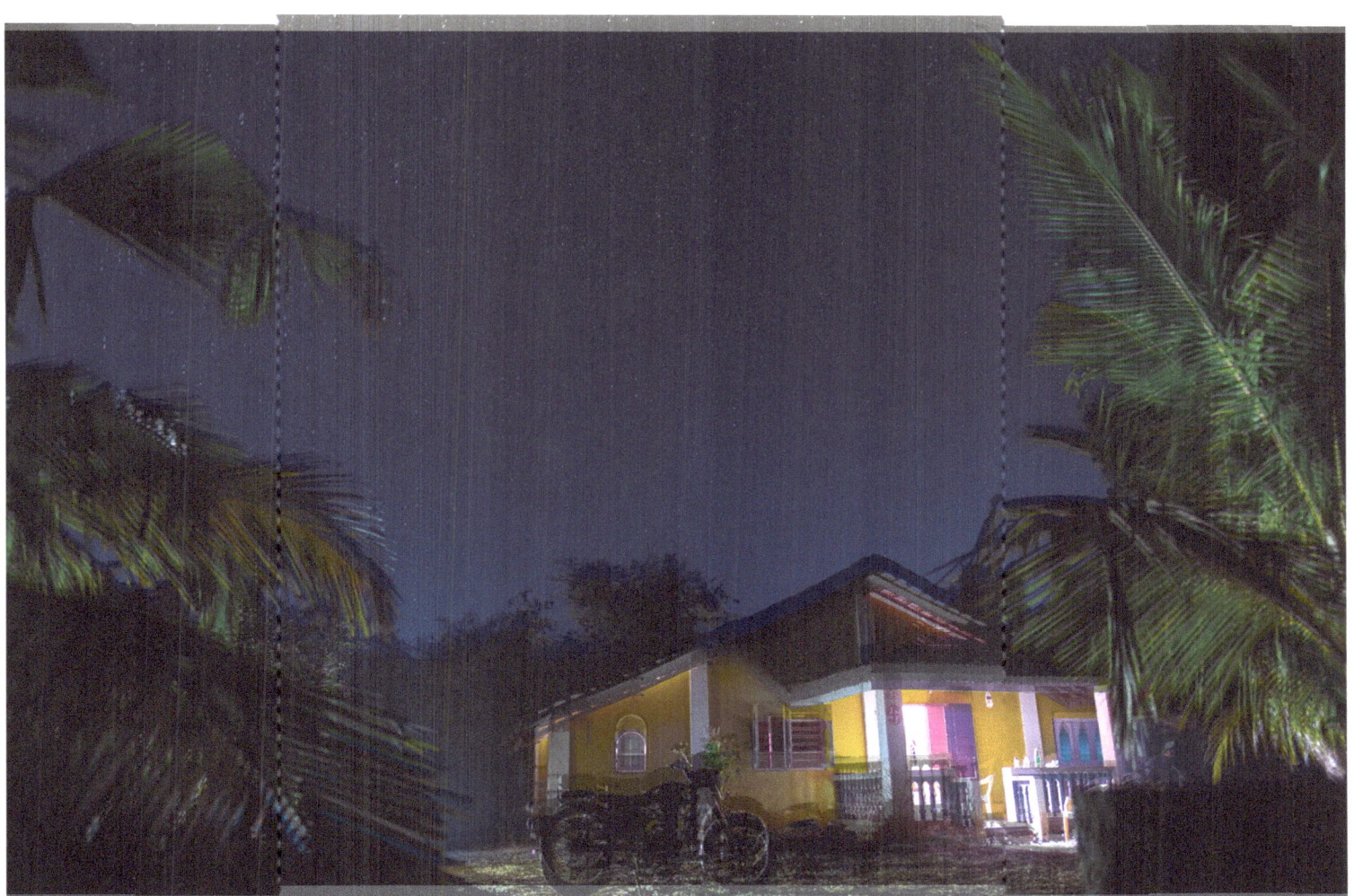

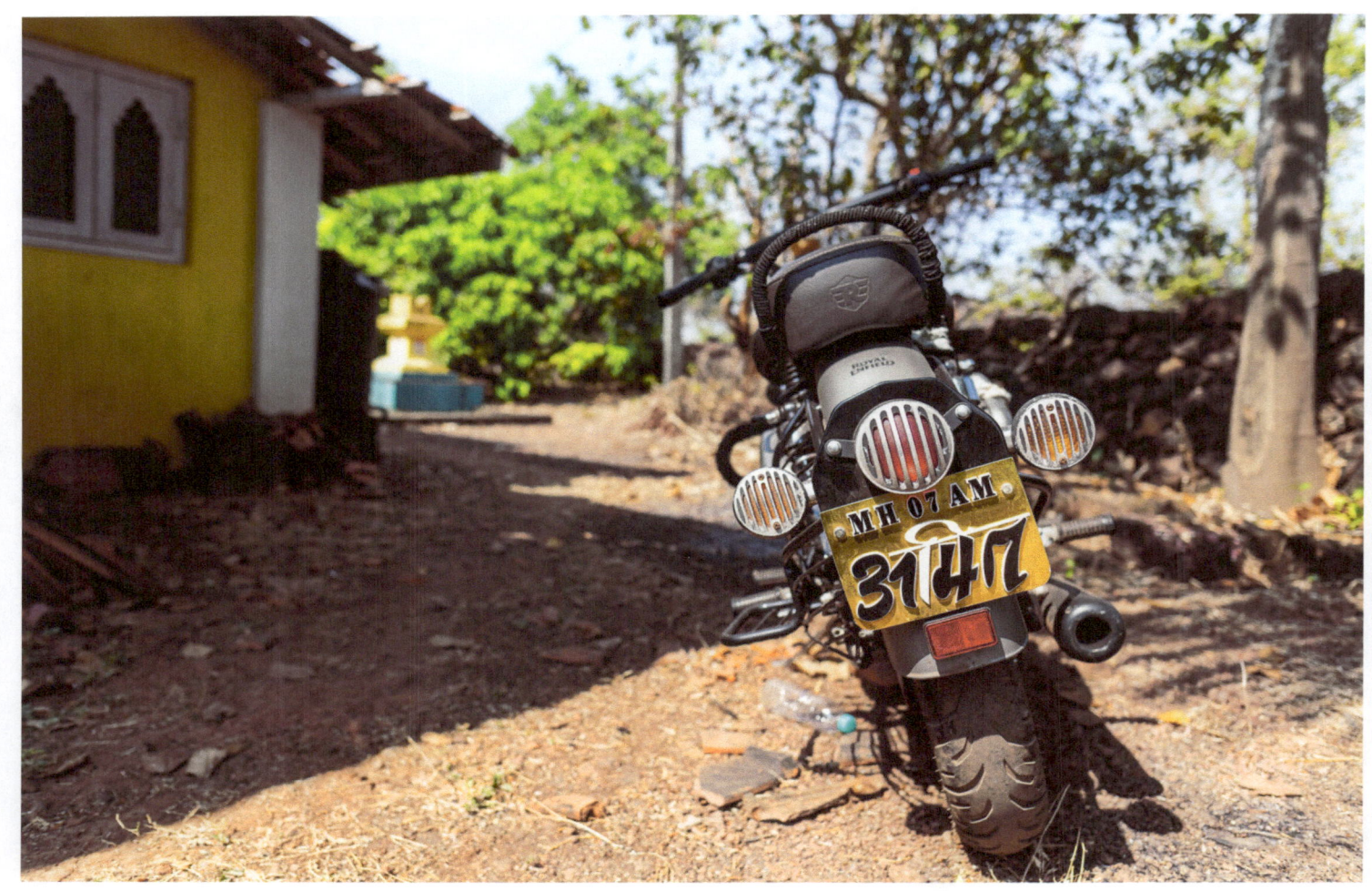

Amit's Bike, Kolamb
Shubham rides his cousin Amit's bike when at his native.
The license plate of the bike, is designed in such a way
that the numbers 3147, translates to 'Amit' in Marathi script.
Malvan, India. February 2020

The Hair Growth Problem, Kolamb
Shubham applies a medicated serum for hair growth,
as he suffers from hair loss due to extensive usage of helmet.
Malvan, India. February 2020

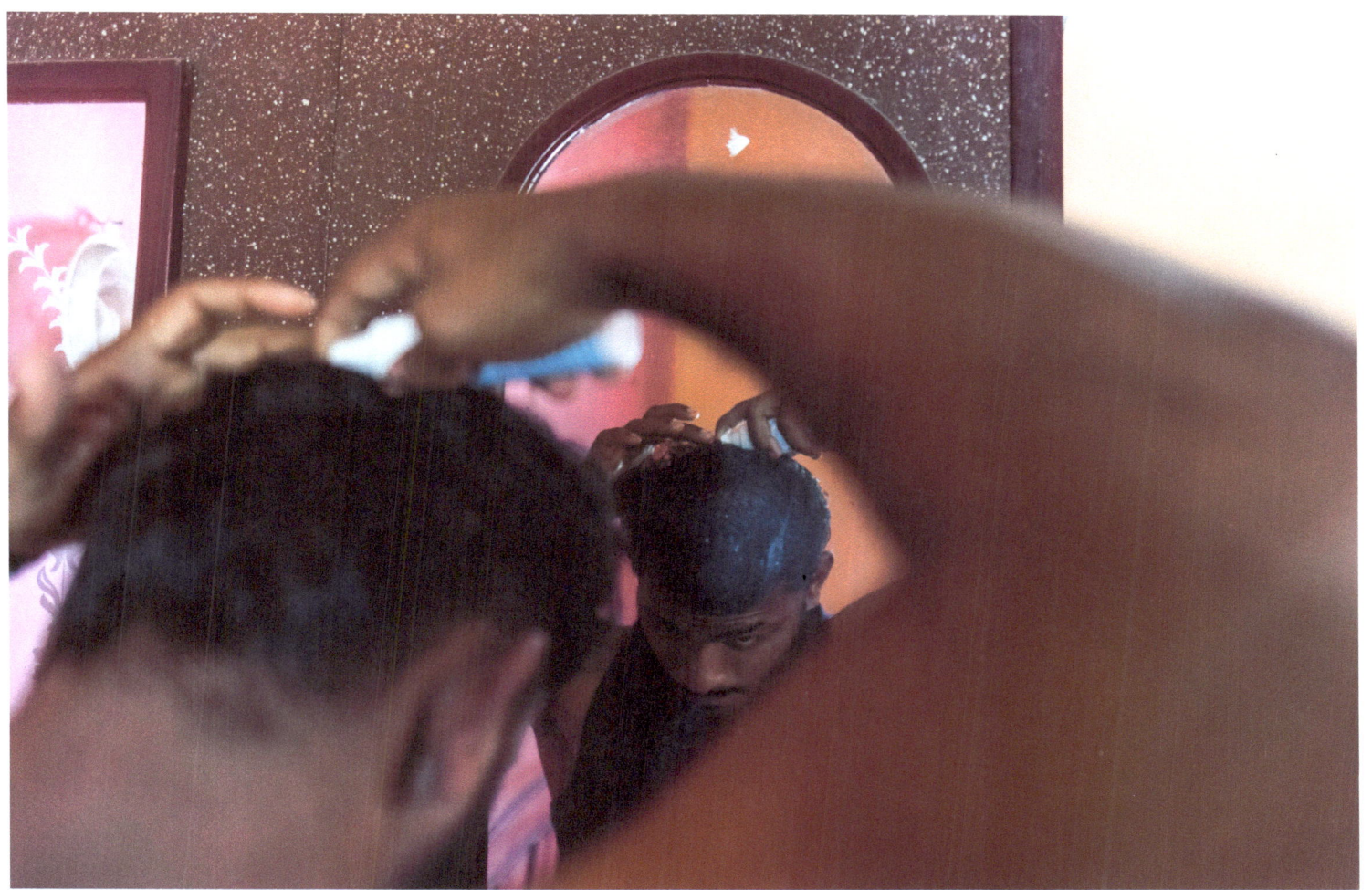

Checking the Mango Tree, Kolamb
Malvan, India: February 2020

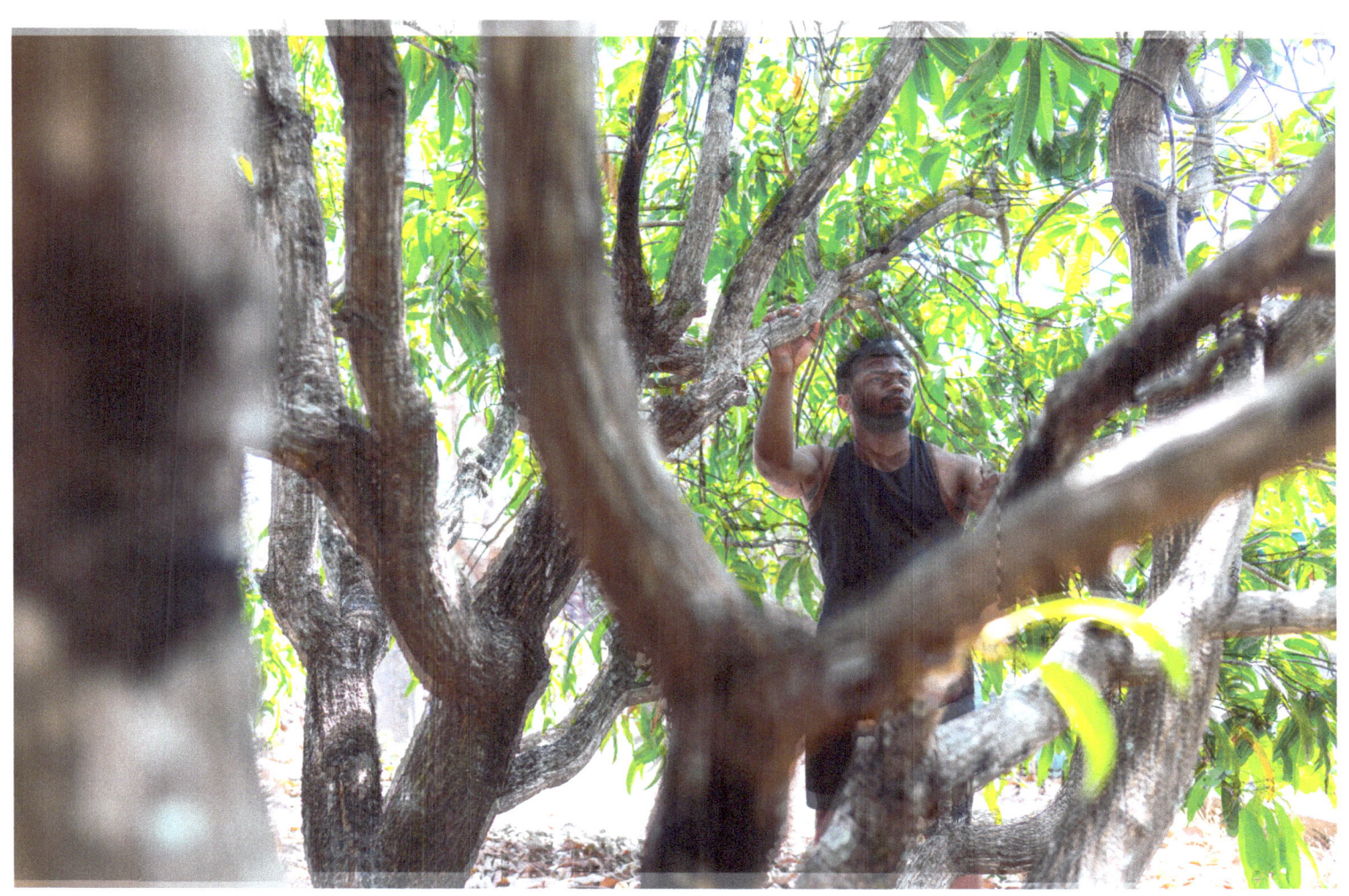

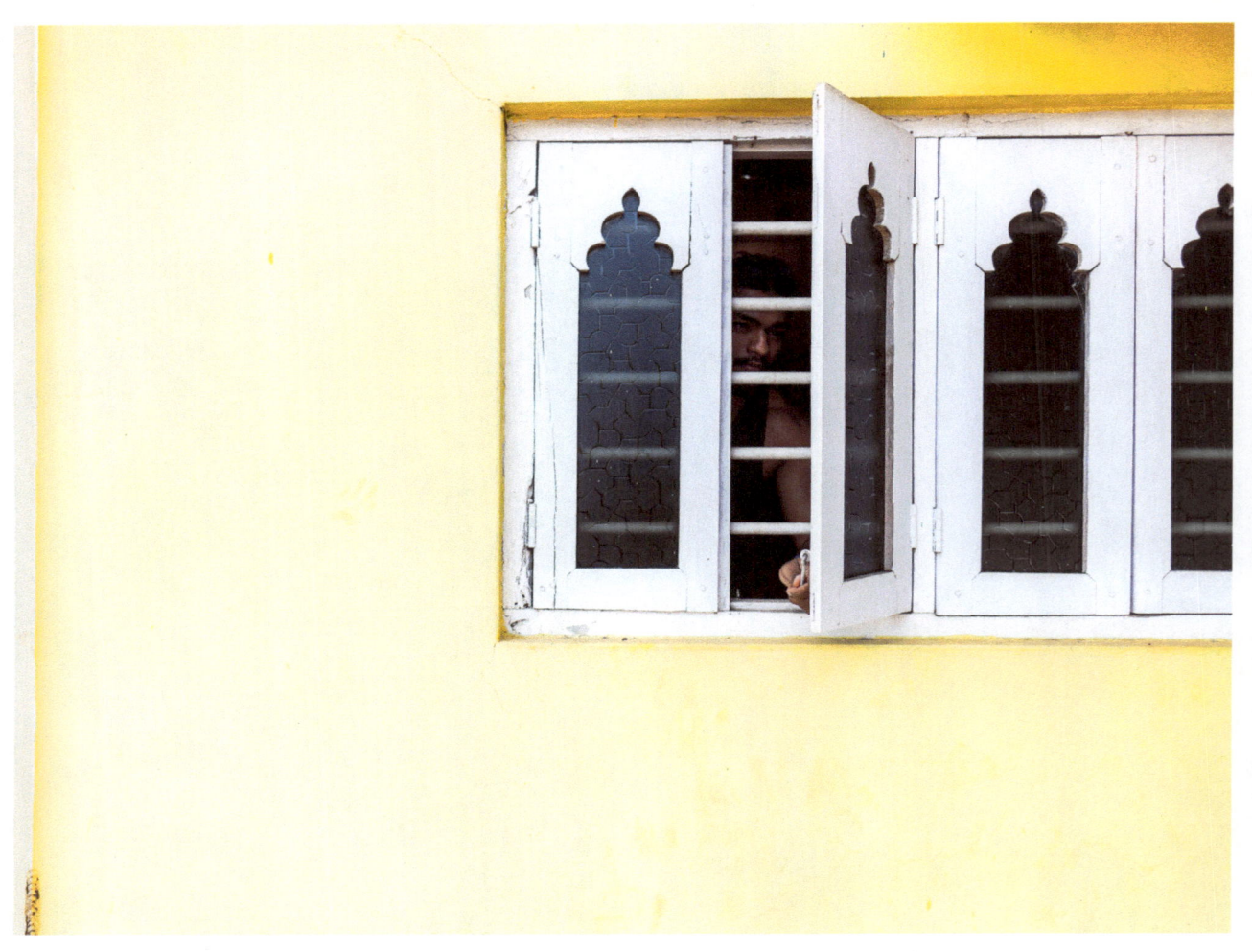

Closing The Windows, Kolamb
Malvan, India. February 2020

Opening The Gate, Kolamb
Malvan, India. February 2020

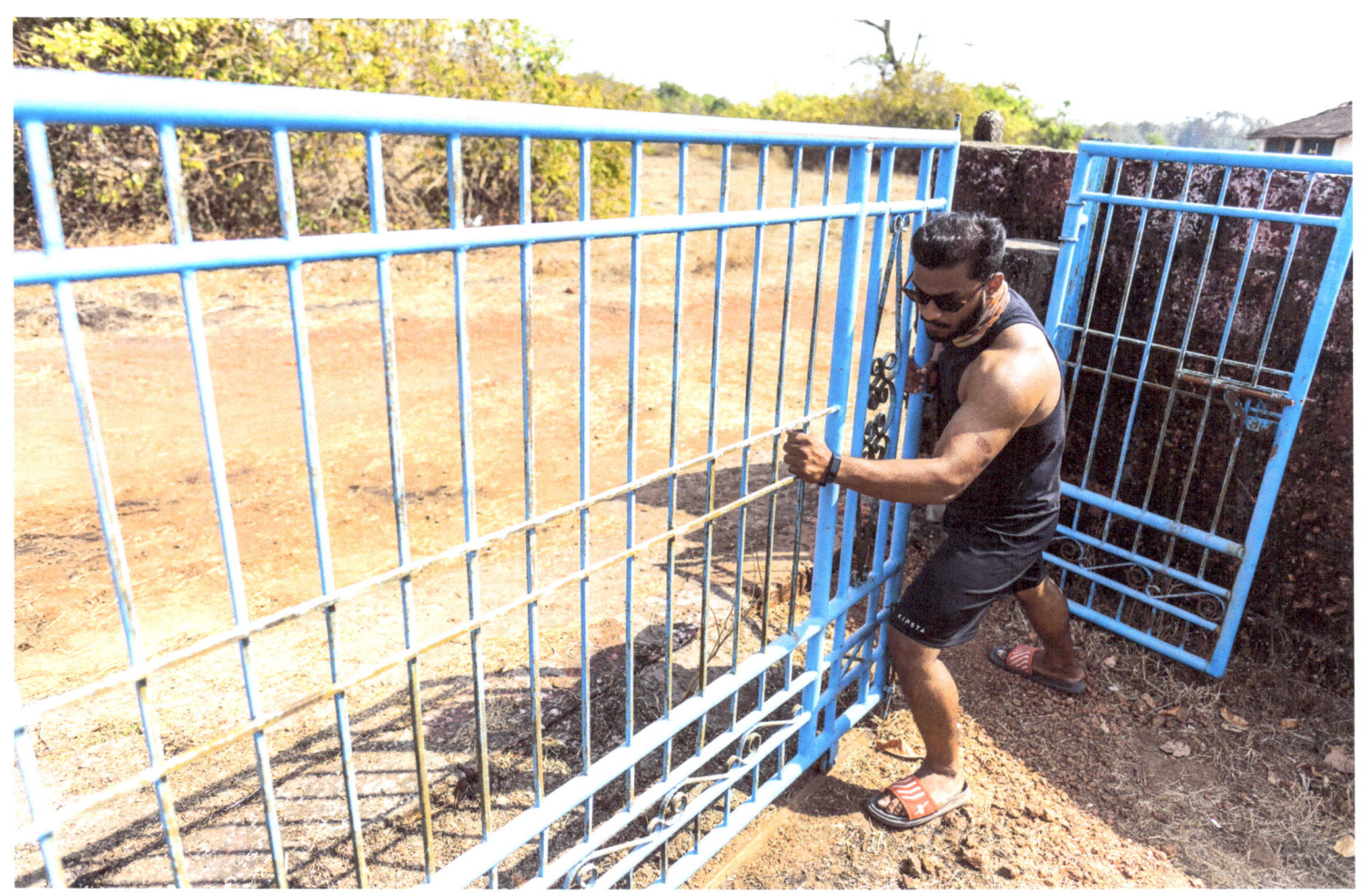

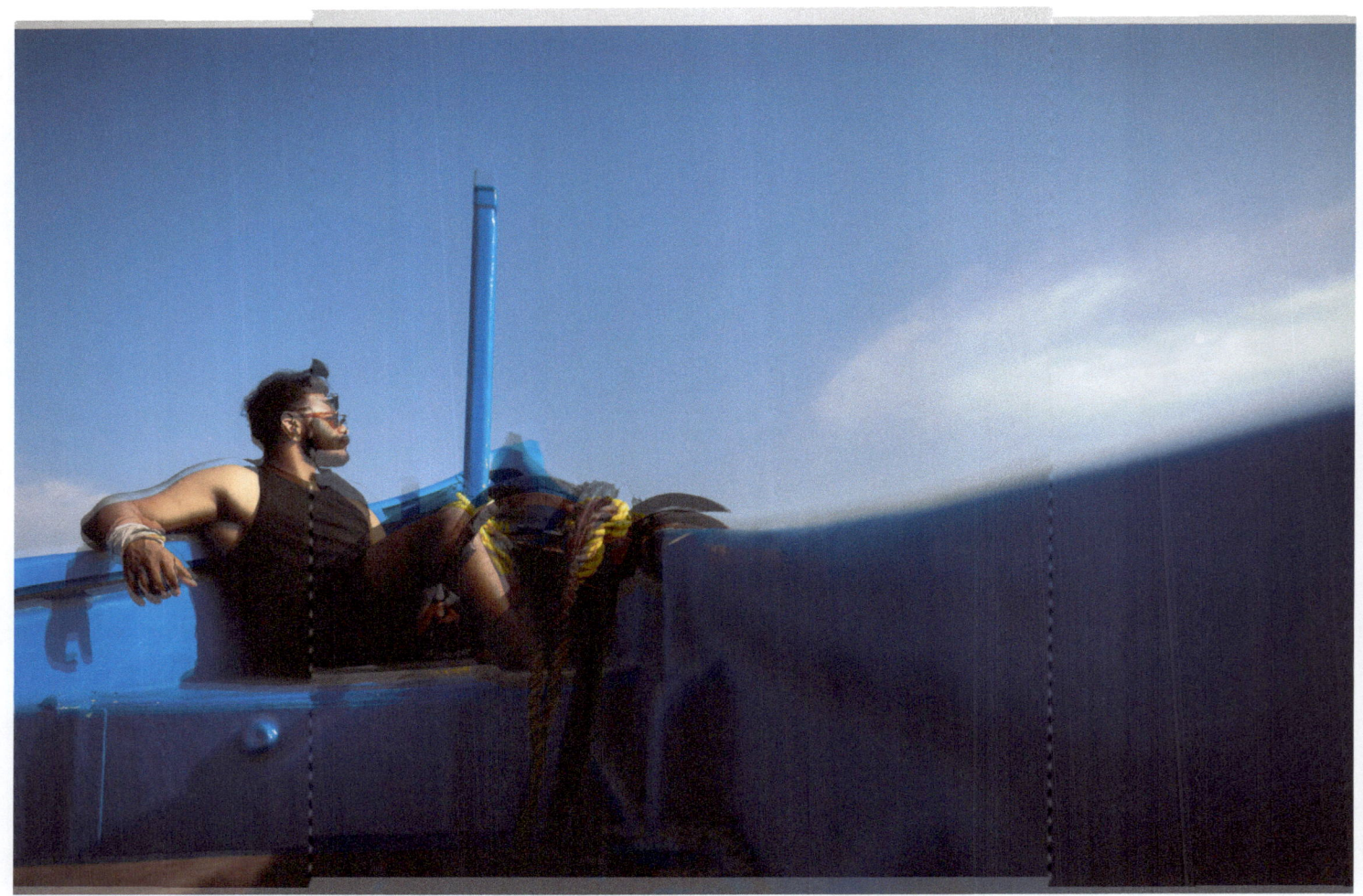

The Boat Ride, Devbag
Malvan, India. February 2020

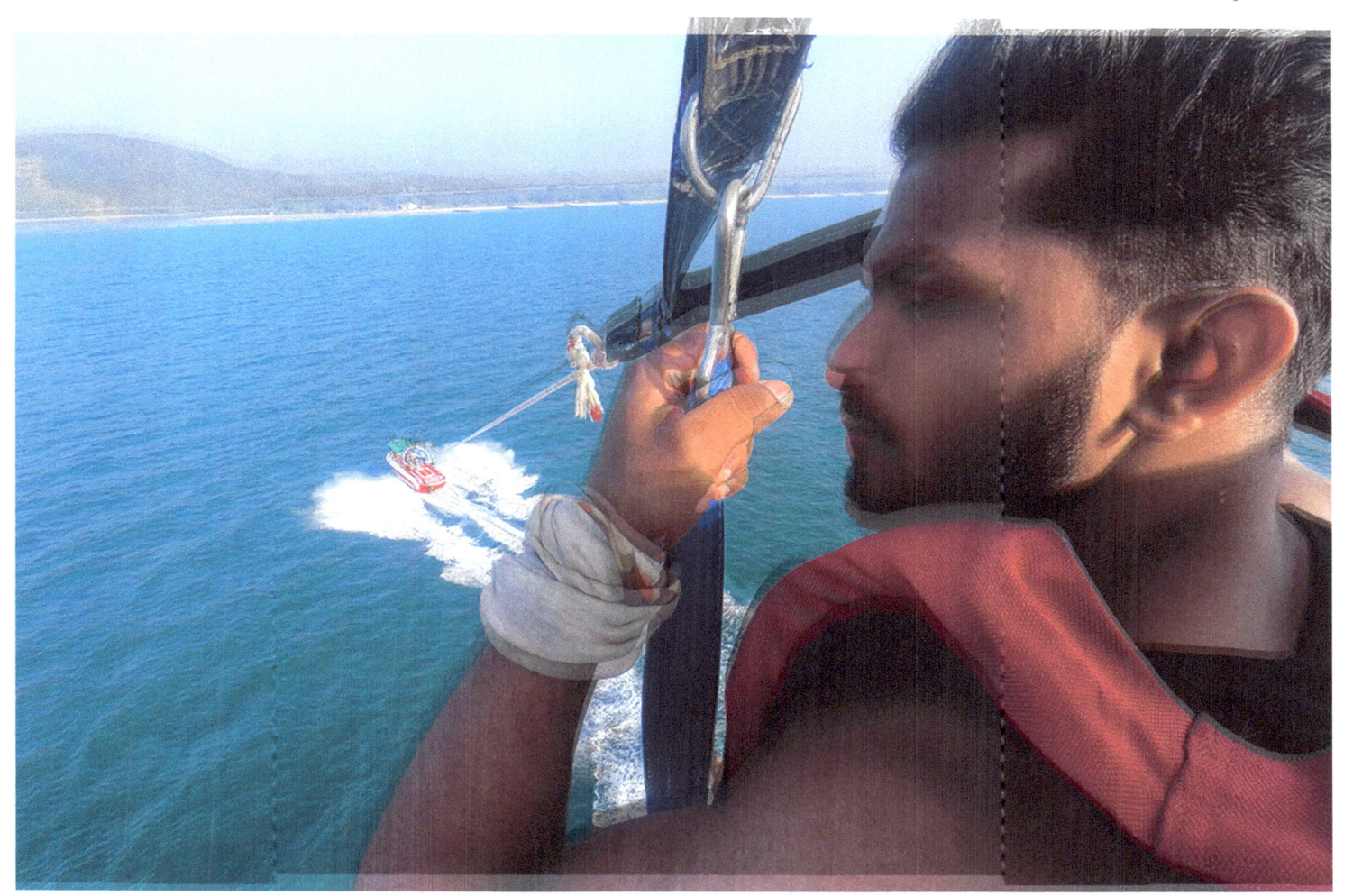

Parasailing, Devbag
Malvan, India: February 2020

Kayaking, Karli River, Devbag (Ariel View)
Malvan, India. February 2020

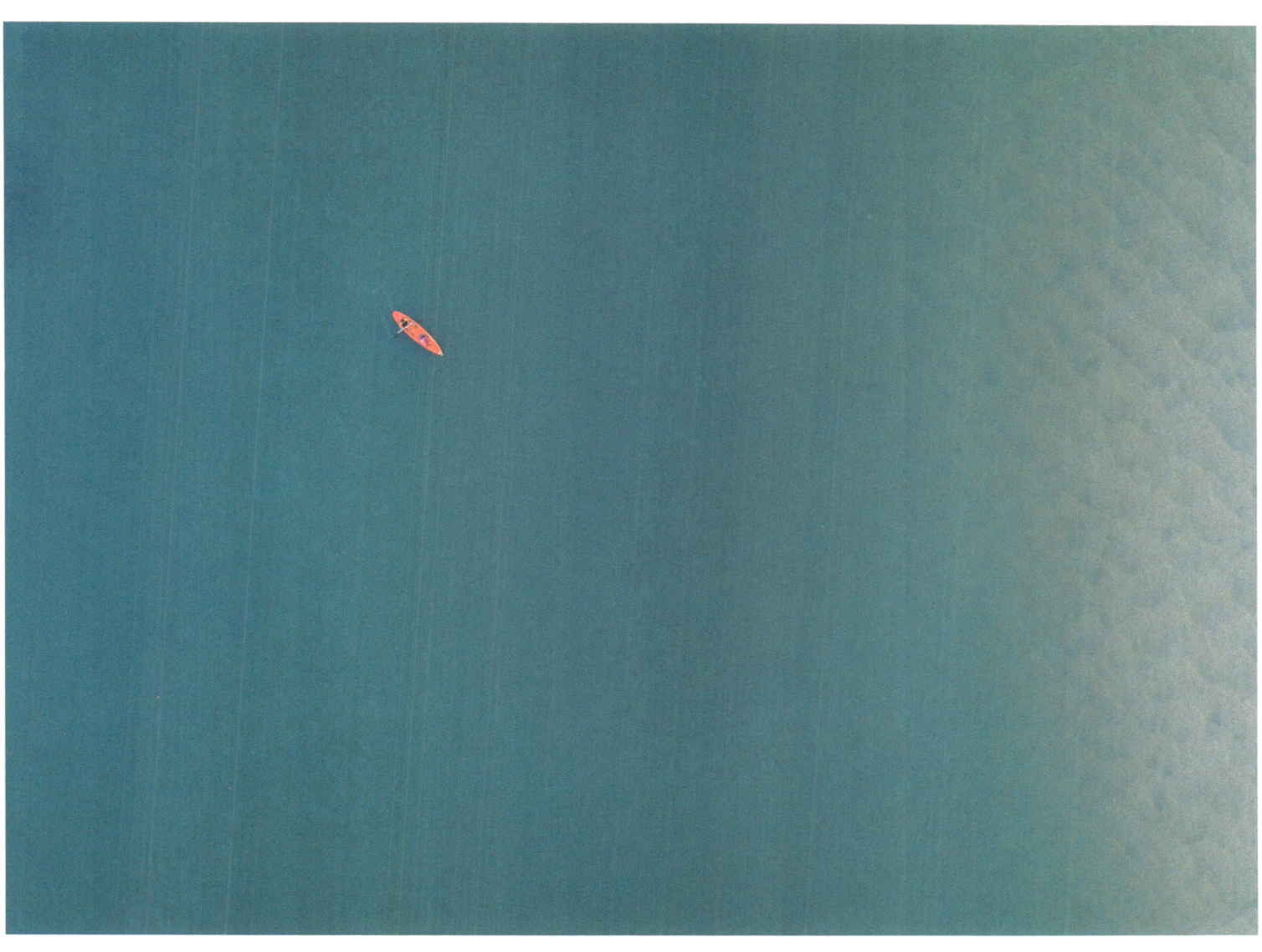

Riding The Boat; Devbag
Malvan, India: February 2020

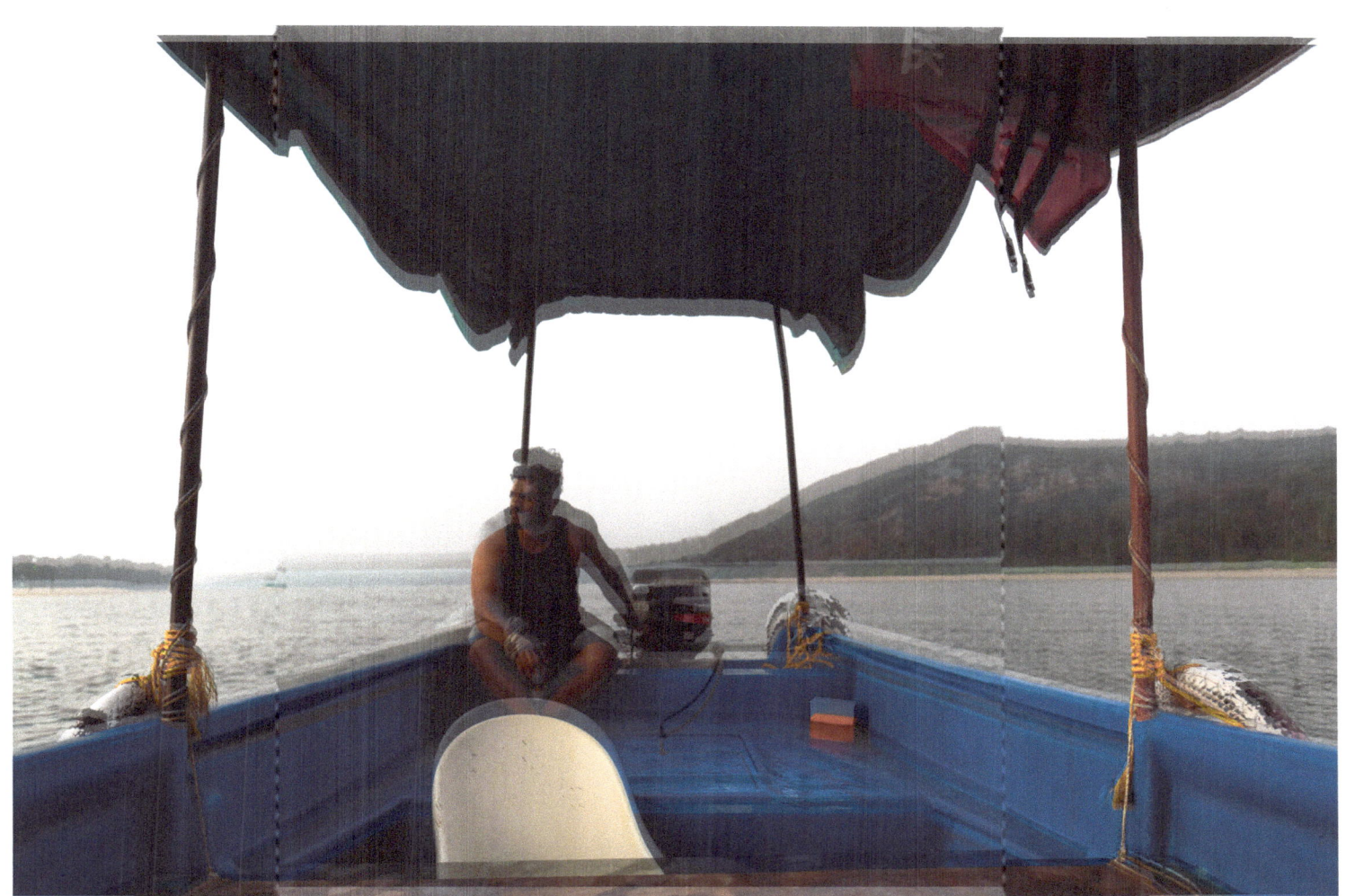

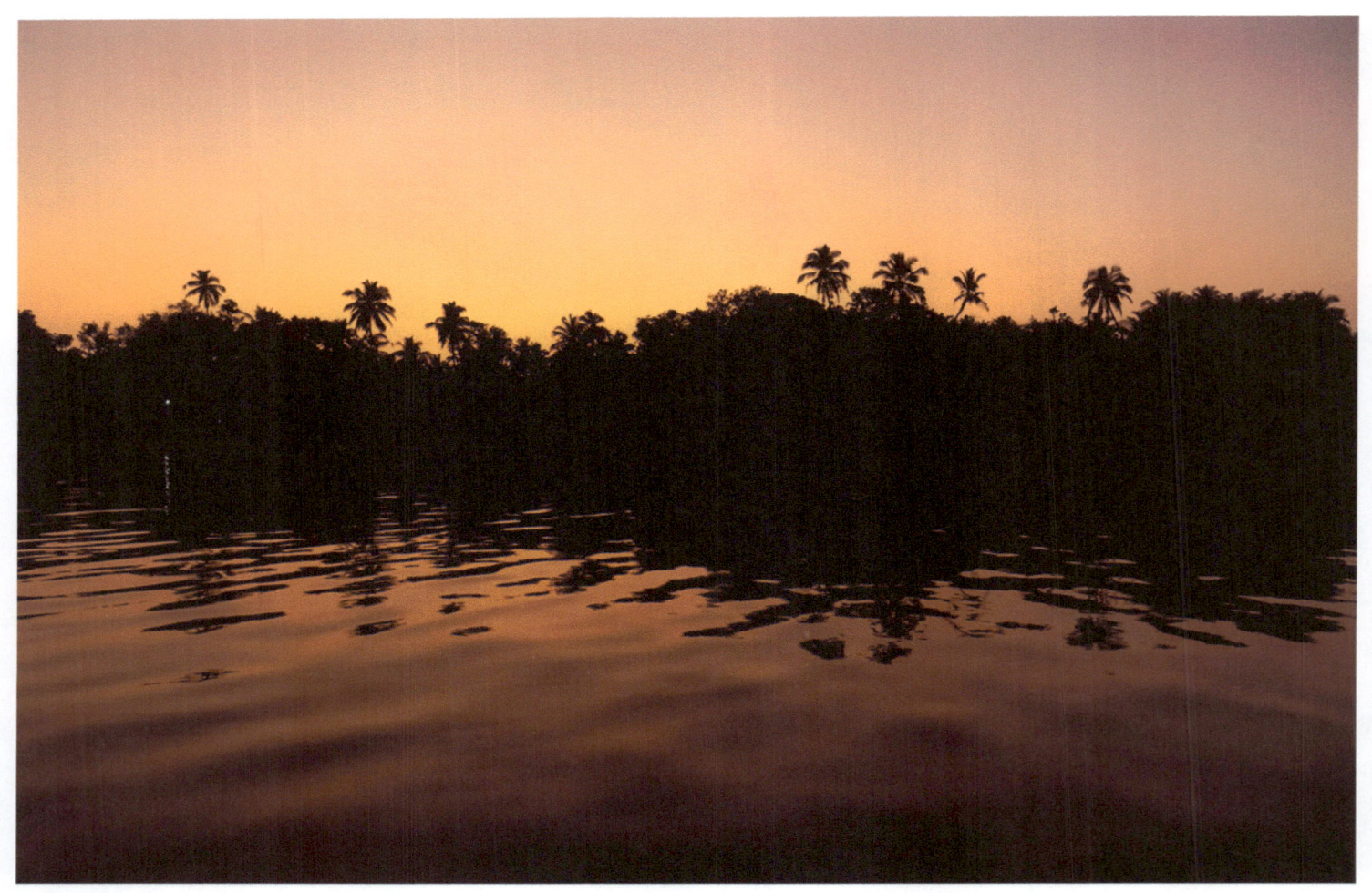

Sunset At Karli River, Devbag
Malvan, India. February 2020

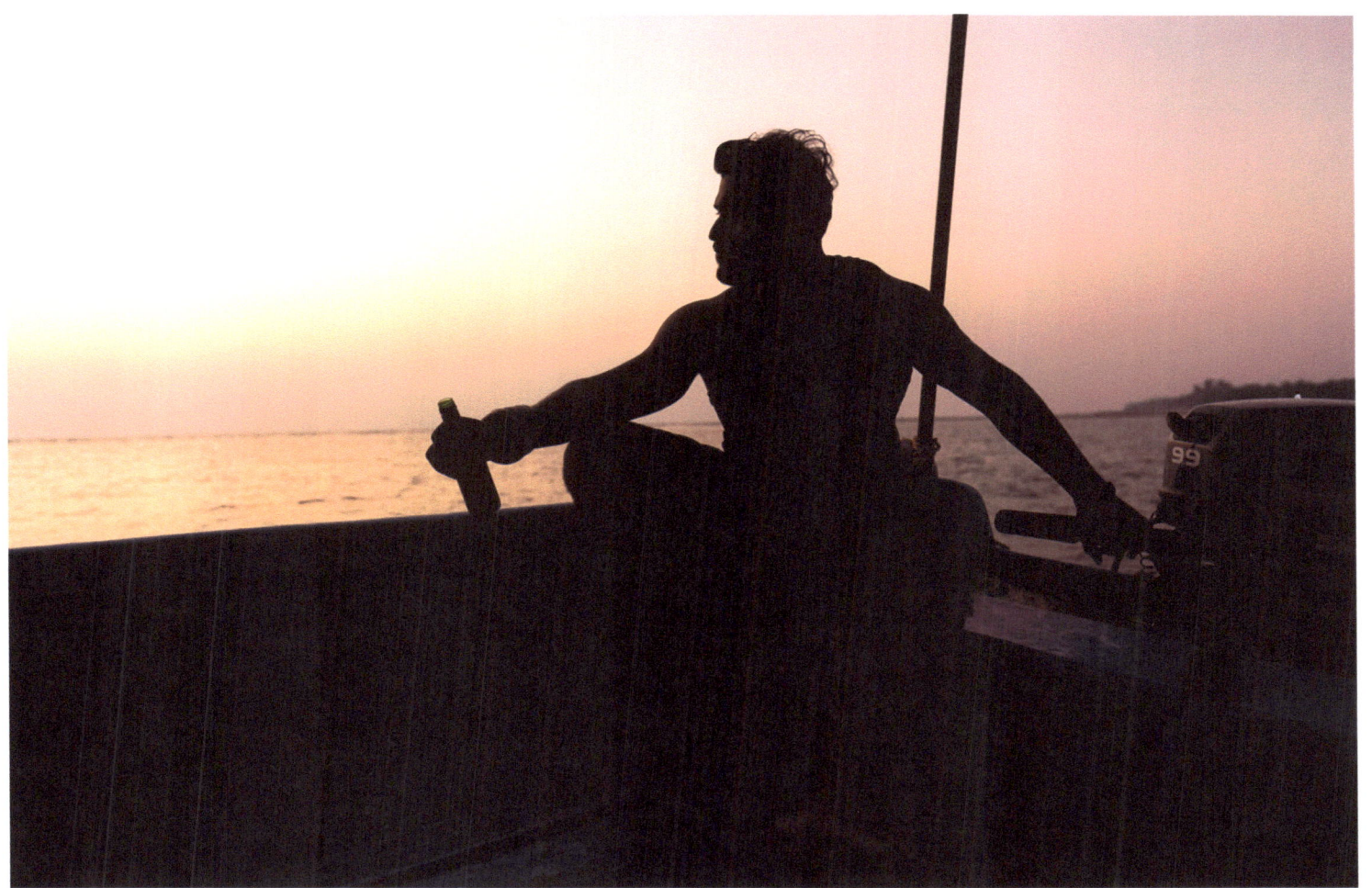

Piloting The Boat, Devbag
Malvan, India. February 2020

The Million Star Hotel, Tondavli
Malvan, India: February 2020

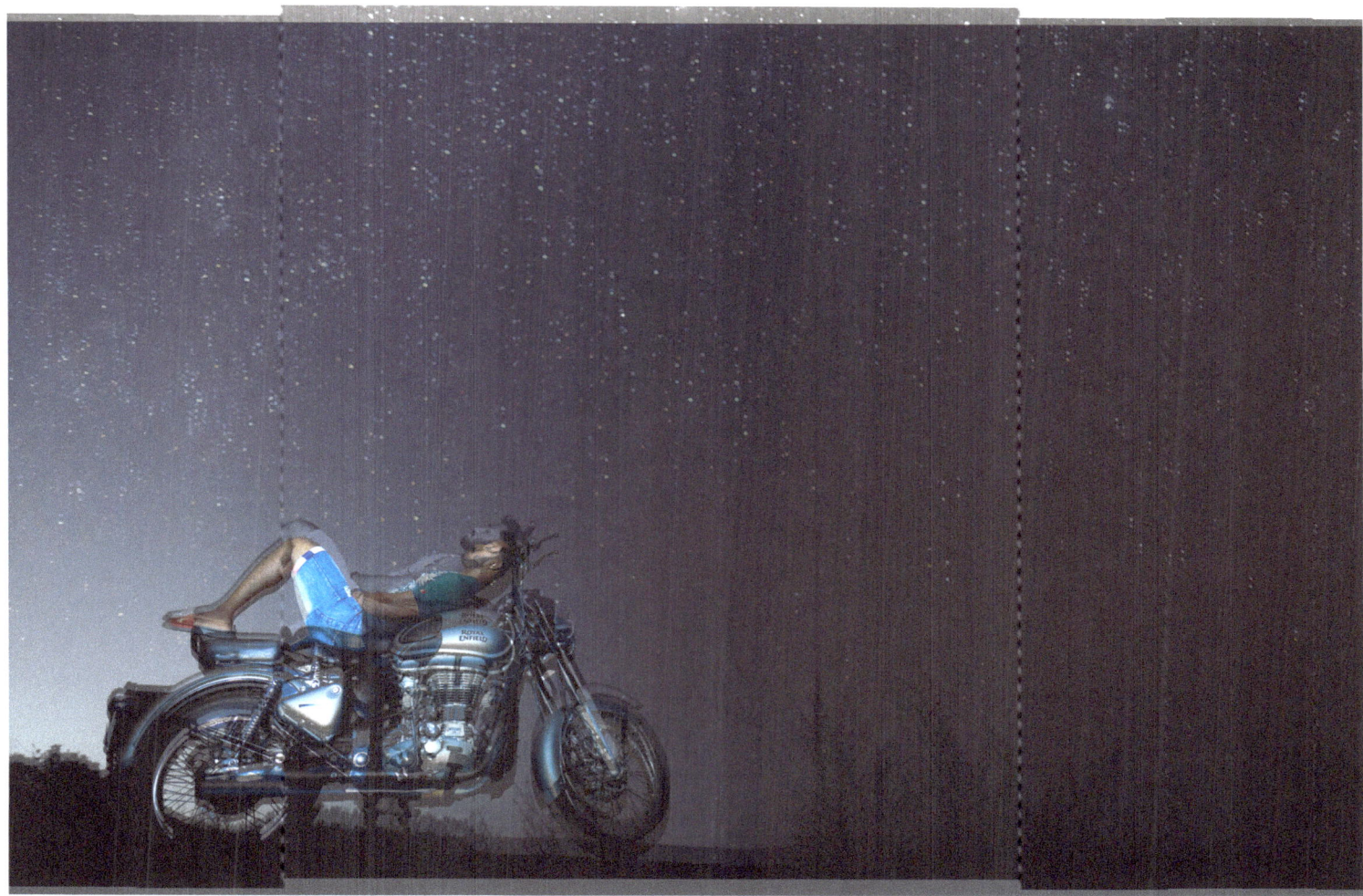

THE SIMPLE PLEASURE
of
BIKE RIDE

www.ingramcontent.com/pod-product-compliance
Lightning Source LLC
Chambersburg PA
CBHW051926210526
45473CB00006B/2153